LIBRARY TRAINING GUIDES

Series Editor: David Baker
Editorial Assistant: Joan Welsby

Introduction by the Series Editor

This new series of Library Training Guides (LTGs for short) aims to fill the gap left by the demise of the old Training Guidelines published in the 1980s in the wake of the Library Association's work on staff training. The new LTGs develop the original concept of concisely written summaries of the best principles and practice in specific areas of training by experts in the field which give library and information workers a good-quality guide to best practice. Like the original guidelines, the LTGs also include appropriate examples from a variety of library systems as well as further reading and useful contacts.

Though each guide stands in its own right, LTGs form a coherent whole. Acquisition of all LTGs as they are published will result in a comprehensive manual of training and staff development in library and information work.

The guides are aimed at practising librarians and library training officers. They are intended to be comprehensive without being over-detailed; they should give both the novice and the experienced librarian/training officer an overview of what should/could be done in a given situation and in relation to a particular skill/group of library staff/type of library.

David Baker

LIBRARY TRAINING GUIDES

Management of training and staff development

June Whetherly

Library Association Publishing

O 23.8
W H E

© Library Association Publishing Ltd 1994

Published by
Library Association Publishing Ltd
7 Ridgmount Street
London WC1E 7AE

First published 1994

British Library Cataloguing in Publication Data. A catalogue record for this book is available from the British Library.

ISBN 1-85604-104-2

Typeset in 11/12pt Palermo from author's disk by Library Association Publishing Ltd
Printed and made in Great Britain by Amber (Printwork) Ltd, Harpenden, Herts.

6/1/94

Contents

 # Introduction

1.1 Overview

This guide presents an overview of how to manage the training of all staff who work in library and information services. It covers any training, development or education of staff. For convenience the word 'training' has been used to cover all three activities.

The guide begins by exploring the purpose of training, and why it is appropriate to take a systematic approach to managing training rather than leaving it to chance. The guide then follows the training cycle of identifying and meeting training needs, and assessing the outcome.

The section on meeting needs describes various training methods which are commonly used. A closer examination is made of the two most popular ones: coaching and short courses. Factors such as whether training should be on or off the job, internal or external, and the use of internal or external trainers are considered. The choice of an external course or facilitator is also discussed.

Throughout, the emphasis is on providing the best conditions for learning, and hence change, to take place. A section on learning sets out to equip the training manager with an understanding of how people learn and what factors affect our ability to learn.

No less important is the development of an understanding of who has responsibility for learning and training. Ensuring the training function has good organization and administration is also vital. There are chapters on both of these topics.

A practical approach has been taken. This is backed by examples of working documents intended to give an insight into how some library and information services tackle aspects of the management of training and staff development.

1.2 The uses of a systematic approach to training

It will be necessary to consider how relevant the pursuit of a systematic approach in the rapidly changing world in which people work actually is. This guide argues that it is desirable to manage training in a systematic manner and that there must be flexibility to allow for accommodation of unforeseen training needs. It is, of course, recognized that much important training and learning takes place informally and without pre-planning.

The systematic approach taken can be applied to services of any size though the solutions are likely to vary. The very small unit will not be in a position to buy in a short course whereas that is likely to be an appropriate way of meeting training needs in a larger organization. The smaller unit may instead place greater emphasis on co-operative ventures and sending people on external courses.

1.3 Identifying the questions for which answers are required

As with most aspects of management there are no 'right answers'. The suggestion that there are answers implies that there must be questions. This text sets out to help readers formulate their own questions and arrive at answers which are satisfactory for themselves and their organization. The necessity to do so was summed up by Charles Handy:

> Later on, I came to realize that I had learnt nothing at school which I now remember except only this – that all problems had already been solved, by someone, and that the answer was around, in the back of the book or the teacher's head. Learning seemed to mean transferring answers from them to me.
>
> There was nothing about change in all of that. Nor, in fact, was there much about learning as it really is. Real learning, I came to understand, is always about answering a question or solving a problem. 'Who am I?' 'How do I do this?' 'What is the reason for . . . ?' 'How does this work?' 'How do I achieve this ambition?' The questions range from the immense to the trivial, but when we have no questions we need no answers, while other people's questions are soon forgotten. (Charles Handy, *The age of unreason*, Hutchinson)

2 What is training and staff development needed for?

2.1 What is training and staff development?

The phrase 'training and staff development' may mean different things to different readers of this guide. Without overemphasizing the terms 'training', 'development' and 'education', some attempt is made here to explain what the author is thinking of when the terms are used.

All three are concerned, when they are effective, with learning. The emphasis for training is learning intended to meet specified objectives, as, for example, 'being able to issue books correctly using the computer circulation system'. Development is concerned with anything which helps the individual grow, learn, and develop personal awareness, including non-work activities. A library assistant given the opportunity to be part of a working party on promoting the service may learn much about marketing and publicity, what they contribute to group work, report writing and so on. Examples of education in the library and information field are a certificate for library assistants or a first degree in librarianship.

The distinction between the terms is often blurred, but dwelling on the definitions will not help an understanding of the management of training and staff development, which is perceived to include all three.

2.2 What happens without training?

Before exploring why training is needed, it is useful to consider what happens without it.

An organization which pays little or no attention to training may exhibit the following symptoms:

- The organization/library service is not meeting its objectives.
- Change is difficult to achieve because staff have got out of or never developed the habit of learning at work.
- A high rate of staff turnover, especially of the able and ambitious, (though this will be affected by the state of the employment market).
- Underdeveloped staff who are not ready for promotion and who feel stuck in the organization and unable to compete for jobs outside.
- Demotivated and disillusioned staff.

Such symptoms are not those of a healthy organization and not surprisingly can lead to a downward spiral – services not delivered, resources reduced, disillusioned staff, 'fire fighting' everywhere, further reduction in services and so on.

Lack of training is not the sole reason for an unhealthy organization. If, for example, the service is held back because there is no vision of what it is about, this is likely to be the result of lack of leadership, not of training.

However, well-managed training can play a significant role in the provision of good quality library and information services.

2.3 What training is needed for

Training can contribute to the health and growth of an organization in the following ways:

- The objectives of the organization are more likely to be achieved if staff are trained to do the job required of them.
- Future service developments can be facilitated by ensuring staff have the necessary knowledge, skills and attitudes needed to implement changes.
- The concept of competition is increasingly significant in all types of library and information service. A well-trained staff delivering the service required by customers can facilitate success in ensuring that the service maintains its competitive edge.
- Quality management has received particular attention in recent years and is underpinned by satisfactory training. (As, for example, to achieve standards specified in a quality assurance scheme.)
- Staff morale and motivation are sustained, especially at times when job and promotion opportunities are limited.
- An organization of which learning is an integral part is better equipped for facilitating change. And as change is ever more rapid the ability to introduce and manage it is essential for organizational survival and growth.

2.4 The wider context

Virtually all library and information services are part of larger organizations and decisions about managing training and staff development within the department will need to be placed in the context of overall policies and practises. For example, if a local authority places priority on introducing equal opportunities policies across the whole organization, this will have implications for training needs in each department.

Beyond the confines of the organization, national, international and professional considerations will also have a bearing on training. Changes in legislation on employment and health and safety may result in staff needing to update their knowledge on these topics; the introduction of national vocational qualifications and continuing professional development (whether compulsory or voluntary) will necessitate reconsideration of current arrangements.

2.5 Developing a commitment to training

Once a commitment to training is made, no matter the origin of the impetus, this is usually written down as a policy, strategy or philosophy of training. Advantages of doing this are: to clarify thinking about training, to obtain acceptance and agreement from within the department/organization and to signal to staff a commitment to provide training.

Such questions as 'What and who is training and development for?', 'How and when will it happen?', 'Who has responsibility for it?', 'What resources are needed and how will they be obtained?' will need to be considered, though they may not all be answered at this stage. For example, a policy may set out what training is required but not the source of funding. Once the library and information service has gained agreement for the policy, a next stage may be putting in bids for resources.

Typically policy documents cover some or all of the following:

- A statement of commitment to training.
- Why training is important (e.g. people are seen as the most important asset of the department; the ability of the service to adapt and respond to change; the necessity of meeting service objectives).
- How training needs will be identified (e.g. annual training and development reports; appraisal interviews).
- Which training needs staff can expect to be met from the resources of the organization. (e.g. the needs of an individual to meet the responsibilities of their current job; an individual's needs, whether or not job specific).
- Who has responsibility for organizing training.
- Individual responsibilities for training (i.e. those of the management, line managers, training officer, each individual member of staff, members of training groups).
- Learning methods which will be preferred (e.g. on-the-job training).
- Priorities for training (though these may appropriately be defined in a training plan produced annually or as required).
- Guidelines for access to resources (e.g. who can attend short courses; how much money will be spent and what time off agreed on particular types of education course leading to a qualification not directly relevant to the applicant's current job). Such guidelines may be set out in a separate document, updated regularly.
- The type of learning environment staff can expect (this is probably most likely to be implicit from what is written in the rest of the document rather than explicitly noted).

2.6 Why training needs to be managed

The arguments for training given above should convince the reader that it is not acceptable for the library and information service to disregard training or leave the responsibility for it to the individual employee.

However, regarding the latter, though no effective training can occur unless there is a willingness to learn, an individual may have different priorities from those of the service for which s/he works. So at one extreme, if resources are managed in such a way that 'first come' are 'first served' (without regard to meeting organizational training needs or the needs of the individual to undertake her/his current job), the outcome may be that resources will be used to further the career of a few individuals to the detriment of others and of the service. At the other extreme the neglect of long-term development needs of individuals may lead to demotivation.

The remainder of this guide explores how a commitment to training can be put into practice.

This chapter set out to:

2.7   Summary

- clarify what is understood by training, development and education;
- explore the contribution training can make to a library and information service;
- consider reasons for, and contents, of policy documents on training;
- identify why training needs to be managed and not left to chance.

3 Identifying training needs

3.1 What is meant by 'identifying training needs'?

To achieve what it sets out to do, an organization requires workers who are equipped with the necessary skills, knowledge and attitudes. Any shortfall in the possession of these qualities will lead to a lower level of performance than desired. This chapter looks at the identification of training needs. Reference should also be made to the separate guide by Michael Williamson on the subject of training needs analysis.

Training texts frequently categorize training needs into three groups: organizational, job or occupational, and individual training needs.

Organizational needs may arise when current objectives are not being met because performance is not satisfactory. For example, a significant increase in complaints about staff behaviour towards users may suggest that staff attitudes are unacceptable or that interpersonal skills need developing.

When new services are being introduced, there are likely to be training needs. For instance, staff may require a greater awareness of the requirements of people with disabilities before they can implement fully a policy decision to develop and improve services for people with disabilities. Any plan a service wishes to make and implement will depend on the abilities of the staff to carry it forward, and consideration of training needs should be made at the planning stage.

Identifying *job or occupational training needs* is a different way of arriving at a similar outcome. A detailed analysis of each job should be made to identify the skills, knowledge and attitudes required and hence what training is needed for the job. A systematic approach to recruitment uses this method to tell potential applicants what qualities the successful candidate is expected to have. Such analysis might be used when there are significant changes to jobs (e.g. when a manual issue system is computerized).

Individual training needs are usually the result of inadequate performance in a particular area of work; the result of job changes or promotions which require the occupant to acquire new skills, knowledge or awareness; or related to ongoing career development.

3.2 Why identify training needs?

It is unlikely that training needs can be fully identified unless a systematic approach is adopted, though the degree of formality used may vary considerably. Once needs are identified plans can be made for meeting them, costs worked out and bids for resources made.

Resources for training are always limited. The main ones required are usually time and money. Achieving the best fit between resources and needs ensures the best use of what is allocated. It also enables whoever manages training to demonstrate the value of a training programme when bidding for resources. Another advantage of a systematic approach to identifying training needs, regardless of which method is used, is that in itself it can be a developmental tool. For example, the introduction of annual staff development and training interviews causes staff to think about the whole issue of training and its relevance to themselves, and reinforces the notion that learning does not stop when they leave school or university.

3.3   How to identify training needs

There is a range of methods for collecting information. These include :

- Examination of existing data (e.g. records of complaints about staff behaviour towards users to determine whether performance has declined).
- Observation (e.g. watching how staff are behaving towards users).
- Questioning (e.g. asking staff who work with the users, supervisors and managers about their perception of the increasing number of user complaints about staff behaviour).
- Interviews (e.g. a manager feeds back to a librarian that s/he has been observed behaving in an unacceptable manner towards users and has also been the subject of several complaints; could training help to solve the problem?).

One theme (customer relations) has been used in the examples given above to show that it may be appropriate for several methods to be used to obtain a comprehensive picture.

Whichever approach is taken, the main resource to the person/people setting out to establish training needs is other people. Managers will know what projects and plans they hope to implement and should have some thoughts about training needs designed to meet existing and future objectives. Supervisors will know which staff are performing well and which are not. Everyone will have some perception of her/his job, and how s/he is undertaking and fulfilling her/his role.

Usually the identification of training needs will be an ongoing pro-active process. However, sometimes it will prove necessary to be re-active.

3.3.1   Identifying organizational training needs

Using the example of a service faced with increased user complaints about staff behaviour as a case study, some ideas on how to conduct a systematic analysis of training needs are outlined.

First of all, the scope and purpose of the analysis should be agreed. Should all aspects of customer relations be covered or the brief be kept fairly narrow to address the increased complaints? Someone must be designated as being responsible for the analysis. S/he may not be the person who does all the work associated with the project, but s/he will need to co-ordinate the work, supervise it, report back on the findings of the analysis and suggest ways of addressing issues raised. In this particular case, would it be appropriate for the line manager of the department experiencing most of the problems to have this responsibility? Might part of the problem be how this manager behaves, or could an 'outsider' – for example, from a central training and personal unit, or an external consultant who has no significant prior knowledge of the department – be a more satisfactory choice?

Some plan of how to conduct the analysis must be made. This needs to keep in focus such practical matters as how much time can be spent on this work, what methods of collecting information are likely to be most useful, how available staff will be to answer questions, and whether one person is to conduct the whole project or there be a team enabling ideas and thoughts to be checked out.

The task of collecting information can now commence. In this instance appropriate methods could include: examination of existing data, direct observation of behaviour (or indirect by using video), and asking questions of a range of staff. Careful thought needs to be given to the choice of methods and their impact on people in the organization. Staff and users finding themselves observed on video (with or without prior warning) might react very negatively.

This process will identify problem areas: for example, that several complaints centre around changes in opening hours which have angered many users; staff on Saturdays are frequently offhand; a significant number of the complaints are about a handful of people; the staff working directly with users feel that they have been inadequately trained in using the new computer system and as a result frequently feel defensive when dealing with users.

One thing to note is that not all the performance problems identified have a training solution. The way staff present changes in opening hours to users could be part of the problem and might be improved by training, whereas reconsideration of whether the hours should be changed again would be a non-training response.

Further investigation will enable clarification of such issues. For instance, though staff have been trained for the introduction of the new computer system, it might turn out that this has been less than adequate because insufficient practice time was built in.

Much information will have been gathered which must be studied and sorted. Conclusions can then be drawn and decisions taken on what training and non-training action is needed. It is likely that producing a written report will be the most useful way of setting out these conclusions.

The contents of the report might identify problem areas, implications for training and non-training action with priorities, and an initial training plan. In the case study a relatively small problem – increased customer complaints – had been identified before the analysis started. This can now be broken down into several smaller issues: changes in opening hours; inadequate training regarding the use of the new computer system; behaviour of Saturday staff; behaviour of a significant minority of staff.

To take the first of these and look at it in more detail, action which does not involve training could be to look again at the opening hours and how these have been announced to both staff and users. Training might be required to ensure staff are fully equipped to talk to users about the new hours, and that the managers involved review what they have learnt from the situation and further develop their project management skills.

Whatever the contents, how the report is presented will affect whether it is acted upon. It is unlikely to be sufficient just to write and send in a report. Additionally, key people need to be encouraged to read and think about it, for the intention of the report is to influence outcomes and gain commitment to further action.

Assuming commitment to further action is secured, the next stage will be to develop a training plan and, if appropriate, also one for non-training responses. The training plan will indicate for whom the training is intended, what the aims of the training are, what methods will be used and a target date for completion. If the main training priority were felt to be equipping staff with appropriate information about the changes in opening hours, then the plan might state that this training is for all staff, and has the aim of 'reducing user complaints about changed opening hours'. Departmental briefing groups would be used and the target date for completion would be one month.

The stages for undertaking the analysis described above are:

- Defining the purpose and aims of the analysis.
- Designating who will be responsible for it.
- Planning the analysis.
- Collecting information.
- Further investigation.
- Interpreting and drawing conclusions from the information.
- Reporting findings.
- Gaining commitment for further action.
- Establishing priorities.
- Producing a training plan (and action plan for non-training interventions)

3.3.2   Approaches and methods

The outline described above is offered as one model of how training needs can be identified (in this case, organizational training needs relating to a particular unforeseen performance problem).

It highlights the fact that not all problems can be solved by training. Inevitably any such process will have wider implications for the organization. Staff perceptions of such an approach to identifying training needs might vary from satisfaction that user complaints were being appropriately explored, to feeling defensive about their own behaviour and making the issue an industrial relations one. Presentation of the needs analysis to staff will be just as important to the outcome of the project as presenting a report to the person/people who asked for it to be undertaken.

The latter will also need to be mindful of the implications for the organization. Well-handled training needs analysis can be beneficial. If poorly handled, it can cause problems. An example of the latter is an organization which decides to conduct an organizational needs analysis by sending staff across all departments (including the library and information service) a questionnaire listing various types of training. The recipients are asked to tick those which they feel would be beneficial to them, and return the form. The outcome is a vast quantity of information, with no precise match between the needs of the organization and the needs of individuals. The organization is overwhelmed by the information and the project stands still. Staff have had their expectations raised yet hear nothing more. In subsequent years it becomes difficult for the library and information service to regain staff interest in training.

3.3.3   Identifying individual training needs

Another issue arising from the case study is the handling of the apparent training needs of an individual as identified by an organizational training needs analysis (in this instance the librarian who has been observed behaving inappropriately and about whom there have been a significant number of complaints). Careful judgement of the situation will be required. Factors for consideration will include whether there should be an interview with the librarian and for what reason, how formal it should be, whether the timing is appropriate, and what impact it will have on the successful implemention of the training plan. An ill-judged intervention could have an impact on the service, the organization and the individual.

This may sound extreme but consider the following scenario. The librarian in question is called into the office of her/his manager, is told that there have been complaints about her/him, that s/he has not behaved well towards users. S/he is not told what behaviour is inappropriate, or asked for a response but are told s/he is going to be booked onto a course and given a set time to improve. The librarian, who has been on the staff for many years and has until now considered her/his work to be satisfactory, is stunned, and this feeling is soon replaced with anger and a sense of being victimized. Other staff get to hear about it and take the librarian's side. Quite quickly the goodwill which a sensitively handled organizational needs analysis had secured is dissipated. Resistance to the departmental briefing sessions about changes in opening hours begins to show; motivation to improve services declines.

It was suggested earlier in this chapter that identifying training needs has the potential for being a tool for development. Managing the identification of training needs and subsequent programmes to meet them requires all the skills needed to manage any change in organizations.

3.3.4 Interviews

Interviews provide a key way in which individual training needs can be identified. They may be called different things – appraisal, staff development, performance interviews – and yet share common features. Some link the management of performance with the identification of training needs. All involve:

- assessment of individual training needs;
- sharing that information in the interview;
- consideration of how to meet training needs.

However, practice may vary depending upon where the emphasis is placed. For example, identification of training needs may be based on self-assessment or on the line manager's perceptions of whether performance is satisfactory. In the first case the individual may complete a staff development and training form. This is used as a basis for talking about existing performance, work objectives to be met in the next year, consideration of future career plans and any ways in which training can help. Alternatively, the line manager may lead by giving feedback to the individual and check out her/his response.

Whether the process is based on self-assessment or assessment by the line manager or supervisor, it is not a once-and-for-all event. Frequently interviews are held only once a year. In between, there should be reviews of whether agreed training is meeting the individuals' needs, and when appropriate performance should be monitored. This does not have to be formal. It is important because it reinforces the significance of the training and gives valuable feedback to the individual.

3.4 Providing training 'just in time'

The approach taken in this chapter suggests that it is desirable for the identification of training needs to be a systematic, though not necessarily formal, process which involves everyone. However, one concern is how such an approach can cope with rapid change if the notion of 'just in time' is prevalent. Might it stifle the successful implementation of change which was not foreseen at the beginning of the planning cycle, because resources have already been committed and staff expectations raised?

3.5 Summary

This chapter set out to:

- define what is meant by identifying training needs;
- consider why it is necessary to identify training needs;
- explore ways of identifying training needs.

4 Learning

4.1 Introduction

Learning is central to all training. For training, when it is effective, enables people to learn and facilitates change in understanding and behaviour. The purpose of training in library and information services is to develop the knowledge, skills and attitudes needed by individuals to undertake their jobs and further their careers, and by organizations to meet their objectives.

For example, managers may undertake a 30-week evening course on counselling to improve their management skills. They may gain knowledge of counselling, learn such skills as active listening, and become more aware of themselves and their values. On return to the workplace they may be more conscious of how they relate to their colleagues. In particular the managers might think through and change how they behave in meetings and consider the appropriateness of using counselling skills as managers.

The ability to learn enhances the quality of life, at work and away from it. Individuals have responsibility for their own learning, for no one can do it for them. It can occur at any time and in any place, and is often informal and unstructured. Learning does not happen once and for all, and is a part of growing as a person and of leading a full life.

There have often been assumptions in organizations that individuals will undertake and be responsible for most or some of their own growth and development. However, as discussed in the first chapter, there are many reasons why it is also important for an organization not to leave training and development to chance.

One significant reason is the constant change in library and information services; for example, in information technology applications. This means that learning needs to be considered as an ongoing and continuous experience, not only for the benefit of the individual, but also for the survival and growth of the organization.

Training can take many forms (see Chapter 5 on meeting training needs). Whatever form it takes, its purpose is to provide an opportunity for learning. Those managing training will find it useful to have some understanding of how people learn and what factors affect their ability to learn.

4.2 How people learn

There are many theories and books on learning. Without delving deeply into these theories, some consideration is given here of the four main ways people learn. They are trial and error, being told, imitation and thinking.

Trial and error. Two examples which are typical of this learning method are:

> 'Whoops, I pressed the wrong button on the computer. What's happening now?'

'I anticipate this meeting will be difficult because of my problems of getting on with the other person. I am going to try harder to listen to what s/he has to say, and see whether the outcome is different.'

Being told. This may include verbal or written instruction, such as reading the *Library Association record* or a memorandum on changes in issuing loan stock, hearing a lecture on total quality management or being told how to enable new users to join.

Imitation. One example is the system of 'sitting with Nellie', which is based on one person learning from the existing practice of the other. Another is new recruits to an organization following the norms of behaviour demonstrated by the others; for example, in how they respond to library users.

Thinking. Typical problems which might be resolved by thinking are :

'How can I reorganize the library shelving system without disrupting the service?'
'What do I need to include in this report to ensure that it is persuasive and I achieve what I hope for?'

Each person will adopt her/his own preferred way of learning. For example, some will ask how to put the paper in the photocopier, but others will read the operating manual or watch someone else. Ways of learning may be combined – as in the second example under *Trial and error* above, when the person intending to try out a different way of behaving at the meeting had thought about it first.

4.3 Factors which affect the ability to learn

This leads on to looking at factors which affect the ability to learn.

Motivation. What motivates an individual to learn may be complex. It could include being rewarded by a pay increment for having passed a first-aid course, having interest kept alive by the skill of a trainer, the satisfaction of gaining new knowledge, or expectations carried over from childhood about the necessity to achieve.

Relevance. Whilst some will enjoy learning for its own sake, most people will wish to see the relevance of gaining new skills and knowledge to what they are doing now or are planning for the future. They are likely to ask such questions as, 'How will that course help me do my job better?', 'How will it help my career?'

Experience. Training in library and information services is of adults, who will have a rich range of experience to draw upon, depending on age, work and life experiences. Acknowledging and valuing the advantages of this experience can encourage learning to take place. Disregarding it can be very discouraging.

Individual differences. Closely related to taking experience into account is having respect for each person as a unique individual. A manager undertaking a staff appraisal might demonstrate this by actively listening to the other person's perception of her/his training and development needs, and then by trying to identify training solutions which match the individual's specific requirements.

Learning environment. There has been much written about learning organizations in recent years. An organization which embodies this concept would be one that actively encourages the ongoing learning and development of all its members. Conversely, the environment can discourage learning. Examples are when attendance on a short course means sitting on uncomfortable seats, when the trainer appears uninterested about whether you have learnt anything, and when your manager's first words after the course are, 'Did you enjoy your day off?' or 'I'm glad you're back – we were really pushed without you.'

Active participation. A range of training methods is available. Some are teacher centred, such as the lecture with no input from the audience; others are learner centred, such as role play or counselling. When learners are encouraged to participate actively, they share the responsibility for the process of learning.

Shared responsibility. Each individual has responsibility for her/his life-long learning. However, in the work context this is shared, and significant messages are given out about these responsibilities. An organization which has a training strategy and plan, and which regularly assesses training needs and ensures that these are met within the resources available, is indicating that training is important.

Sense of progress. How often is the complaint made that 'No one tells me how I am doing my job'? A vital aid to learning is the provision of regular feedback on progress, whether that is on a training course or in the routine performance of a job. In recent years there has been greater emphasis on appraisal and performance review. Learning is likely to be facilitated when the responsibility for assessing progress can be shared between the organization and the individual, such as by using an appraisal system to identify training and development needs, which requires input from both.

4.4　Learning as a complex process

How we learn and what factors affect our ability to learn are complex matters. For example, one person came to regard her preferences for learning in a group as being actively participative and drawing heavily on her own and other people's experience. When she attends lectures she has often found her attention wandering. Yet the same person was surprised at how hard she concentrated and worked when attending a short course on finance when the trainer 'talked at' the group for two whole days. On that occasion the participant's dislike of this method was overcome by strong motivation to learn.

4.5　Summary

This chapter has focused on:

- learning and change as an outcome of training;
- the main ways in which people learn;
- factors which affect people's ability to learn.

5 Meeting training needs

5.1 Introduction

There are many methods of meeting training needs: far too many to document here. However, some of the most popular methods are noted and some thought is given to current developments in the field. Two well-used methods: coaching and short courses, are described in greater detail to tease out some of the factors to be considered: preparing training; skills of trainers; whether to hold training in-house or externally, on or off the job; whether or not to use an external facilitator; what to think about when using an external provider.

5.2 Coaching

5.2.1 What is coaching?

The literature on the topic of coaching can be confusing. Common themes seem to be that it is about helping a colleague to undertake a task or solve a problem, with the result that the learner is better able to do so than would otherwise have been the case. Approaches include planned tasks, discussion, advice and feedback on performance.

Some texts focus on learning how to do tasks which are repeated, such as procedures for notifying a user that a reserved book is ready for collection; others on one-off problems, such as how to handle a specific staffing issue.

Another dimension is the identification of a training need/problem and the provision of the solution. In induction training for a new member of staff who has no knowledge of the computer issue system the coach is likely to identify both. The coach might explain and demonstrate how it works and ask the learner to practise. Alternatively, it could be the learner who identifies both problem and solution, for example when there is a problem with a particular member of staff which they are not sure how to handle. The learner may seek out assistance from her/his line manager, who by listening, using other counselling skills and giving advice when requested helps the learner to tackle the problem in her/his own way.

In other situations these roles are shared. For example, the coach recognizes that a librarian is not always being as helpful as s/he might be to users. When the librarian complains about a recent situation in which a user was difficult with her/him, the coach uses the opportunity to discuss the matter with the librarian and help her/him work out how to avoid such situations. This might include how the librarian could be more helpful. Someone newly appointed recognizes that s/he does not know enough about how to manage the financial part of the work. S/he seeks out help from her/his manager, who provides explanations and advice.

| 5.2.2 | ## Advantages and disadvantages of coaching |

The main benefits of coaching are that it directly and realistically relates to a job to be done; it can be tailored to the needs of each learner, including adjusting the pace for each person; and opportunities for coaching can more readily be found than for off-the-job training. The last is particularly true in libraries and information services as it is often difficult to release learners for significant periods of time, and because staff work when courses or other training events are not always readily available. Additionally, coaching can enhance the relationship between the learner and the coach (who is usually her/his manager or supervisor), develop analytical and interpersonal skills in both coach and learner, encourage involvement and innovation, and provide an opportunity for learning from successes and failures, as well as a mechanism for delegation.

The main disadvantages are that it requires skilled coaches and is time consuming.

To illustrate these points two examples are given; one relating to a unique problem, and the other to training for a repeated task.

A middle manager seeks help with a problem on which s/he has become totally 'stuck'. It is the type of problem for which there are no right answers, and an appropriate way of helping might be to get the middle manager to talk it through while the coach listens, asks open questions, summarizes what has been said – in other words helps the learner to explore the problem so that s/he can arrive at a new understanding of it and deliberate on possible solutions, with a view to being able confidently to make a decision on how to tackle the problem. If instead the coach, though s/he has agreed to help the manager work out a solution, is pushed for time, not prepared to listen, wants to give unwanted advice and interrupts with 'I would do it this way', it could turn out to be a demotivating experience rather than a learning opportunity.

A coach is preparing to train a new library assistant on the computer issue system. To make the session most effective the coach will need to consider such factors as what knowledge and experience the library assistant has of such systems, what might be covered in the session and how the contents will be ordered, and also the date, time and venue, intervals between coaching, any necessary administrative arrangements, how the session will be reviewed, and what needs to be prepared in advance. Assuming a computer terminal is set up, the session may proceed as follows. The task is introduced and demonstrated to the learner, who is asked to explain it in her/his own words and then practise. When the learner has practised sufficiently the coach might demonstrate at full speed and ask her/him to try again. All this might be related appropriately to another aspect of using the system.

In both examples, time and many skills are required of the coach. One key skill is the ability to give feedback on how the learner is performing, which will enable her/him to have a sense of progress – 'You are accurate though at this stage you are not fast enough. You are following the procedure in the correct order.' To reiterate, effective coaching is greatly dependent on the skills of the coach.

| 5.3 | ## Mentoring |

Mentoring is closely related to coaching. A part of mentoring is to encourage the learner to identify problems and solutions and hence it requires similar skills to those used in coaching. Often the mentor will be the line manager, though for senior staff it can be appropriate for someone outside the organization to fulfil the role. The mentor will not only be concerned with helping to solve problems but also with assisting in developing and meeting longer-term career plans and goals. A separate guide, written by Biddy Fisher, covers this important topic.

5.4 Job rotation/Secondment/Shadowing

All these provide the opportunity to learn by directly undertaking tasks or a job which is new, or by observing how someone else does a job. A library assistant, having spent six months learning basic procedures in the adult lending library, may then spend a period of time providing services to children. A librarian may be seconded to another organization for a year to undertake a research project. A potential manager is given the chance to observe what a senior manager does by shadowing her/him for a day or week and having the opportunity to talk to the senior manager about this experience and what s/he has learnt. The senior manager may learn as much as the designated learner.

5.5 Project work/Consultancy

Often a specific project is tackled by asking one person or a group to work on it. Possible options may include working out new policy initiatives, planning the reorganization of the information desk, and publicizing a new range of activities for children. Whereas project work might introduce the learner to entirely new knowledge, experience and skills, consultancy is more likely to involve going into a situation as an 'expert' and learning by applying what is already known (e.g. advising another department on how to organize its stock or facilitating the senior managers in another library service to enable them to review how they work together).

5.6 Group work

So far the emphasis has been on meeting the training needs of the individual. Groups also have needs, which must be met if they are to develop and be maintained. For example, a team recognizes that it is not functioning effectively and asks for help to tackle unresolved conflict; or a group, newly established after a restructuring, seeks assistance with team building.

Training groups which meet regularly also offer learning opportunities. An example is an action learning set comprising managers from different library and information services which convenes monthly. It provides a 'safe space' for one person to explore and work with a problem or issue. In addition to gaining insights into the particular problem, the whole group has the chance to develop counselling skills, undertake group process work, learn more about how groups work, and gain greater personal awareness.

5.7 Library and information conferences/meetings/lectures/exhibitions

Attendance at such gatherings provides the chance to meet colleagues who work in the same field both formally and informally. This can be invaluable for finding out how other organizations and individuals tackle similar issues, for updating knowledge when contributors and speakers are leading practitioners or theorists in their subject area, for seeing and trying out the latest equipment and for identifying potential sources of help.

Such gatherings offer other opportunities to learn and practise skills. Active membership of a professional body could involve organizing a conference, or publicizing it, or presenting a paper, or being a helper on the day.

5.8 Visits to other library or information services or related organizations

Seeing what happens elsewhere, meeting and talking to the staff in the organization as they go about their work, and discussing what has been seen and heard offer similar opportunities for learning to those outlined in the previous section. In particular, it can introduce staff to other approaches and systems. This can be useful for gathering information, facilitating change and encouraging reappraisal of existing practices.

5.9 Guided reading

This can cover any relevant literature, including keeping up to date with library and information journals. The greatest impact is likely to be achieved when what has been read is then discussed.

5.10 Library, information and other education

Many staff will have a first-degree/library and information qualification before they join the organization for which they are currently working. However, some courses are likely to be undertaken while staff are in a job, by using day release or distance learning. Examples are those which lead to a certificate for library assistants, a higher degree in the management of library and information services and a master's degree in business administration – all of which could be preparatory to earning promotion.

The needs of support staff may also be met by undertaking a course leading to a qualification; for example, a certificate in training and development for a training officer.

5.11 Open learning

Some topics which occur in virtually all library and information services may lend themselves to open learning. For example, a project initiated by the Northern Training Group[1] and concerned with training public library staffs has identified *Financial management, Enhancing services for disabled library users* and *Dealing with difficult situations* as three topics which could be tackled using open learning. The last two are offered in conjunction with local workshops. Training materials targeted to library and information services are one method of meeting training needs which has potential for further development.

5.12 Computer-assisted learning

This is another area which has much potential for development. One such application could be a customized introduction for new staff to computer issue and other systems. This could prove to be a more cost-effective method than providing individual coaching or short courses.

5.13   Short courses

This is a well-used method. Courses can be in-house or external, run by in-house or external trainers, and be learner or teacher centred. Fundamental to all are factors such as how they are designed, planned, implemented and validated.

5.13.1   Designing courses

Assuming that training needs have been identified, the next stage is to formulate aims and objectives. The aims are used to indicate what the trainer expects to be able to achieve by the end of training and might be general in scope and use unquantified terms: for example, 'To enable participants competently to issue and discharge books.'

Objectives give detailed information about what participants will have the opportunity to learn during the course and also what the participants are likely to be able to do after training. It is desirable, though not always possible, that they should include the following elements:

- The performance that is required of the participant: for example, 'At the end of training the participant will be able to handle all aspects of issuing and discharging books including interlibrary loans, reservations, payments for damaged books and dealing with lost tickets.'
- The conditions which will operate when the performance is being carried out: for example, 'in a busy library'.
- The minimum standards which the performance must achieve: for example, 'accurately and quickly'.

Once aims and objectives are agreed, consideration can be given to the contents and their sequence in the training. Many different approaches might be taken to meet the same objectives, especially when it is not easy to be precise about them. For example, enabling participants to 'gain an understanding of factors which affect learning' might be achieved by presenting a model or theory of learning styles, or by drawing on the experience of the people present regarding how they assimilated particular knowledge or skills, or by identifying environmental factors. Closely associated with content is choice of method and aids. A vast range of methods exists, which includes role playing, discussion, exercises, lectures, syndicate groups, case studies, use of video and computers, questionnaires, and brainstorming. Training aids include flip charts, overhead projectors, television, slides, hand-outs, white boards, manuals, prepared charts and many other possibilities.

The design process is concerned with working out how to meet identified training needs by establishing the purpose of the training, the content, and the training methods and aids to be used. It is also important to build in some way of validating whether the objectives are being met, such as allowing time for giving and receiving feedback as the course progresses.

5.13.2   Planning and implementing training

Factors to be considered are:

Who are the participants and what is their 'entry behaviour'? This covers important matters such as what participants already know, what they can do now and what their motivation is for attending the course. Ideally people should only be present if they positively want to be, as clearly no one can be forced to learn. However, someone may attend less than willingly and come away having learnt a great deal.

How should the learning group be structured? For example, how big should it be, will it consist of staff who are all on the same grade and in the same role or not? A course which sets out to be participative and experiential is not likely to be successful if there are too many participants, because not everyone will feel able to contribute. A good group size for such work is 8 to 12 participants to 1 trainer. Once the group goes over 20 it will be more suited to a teacher-based approach.

What the course contents should be. This is determined by defining them in greater detail and deciding on their sequence.

The venue, dates, times and any intervals in training. Administrative arrangements.

Production of a programme.

How to assess the course. (See the next chapter.)

Preparation of the trainer for implementing the course. This could involve checking all hand-outs are accurate and up to date, or preparing a checklist of ideas expected to arise from a discussion, or an external trainer being briefed on recent relevant developments in the organization.

Constraints. Factors such as the size of the training budget, the skills of the trainer and suitable training rooms all affect the outcome.

The overall approach in this text is to consider training in a systematic way, presenting one stage at a time: identifying training needs, designing training to meet them, planning and implementing the training and evaluating it. The reality is that there is considerable overlap. It might be agreed that the training needs will be met by a course, the contents of which will be topics A, B, C and D. It would be wasteful to design a course including all these topics and lasting two days if it were only discovered much later that staff could only be released for half a day, and that of the four topics it was only essential for B to be covered.

5.13.3 Teacher- or learner-centred courses

In recent years the trend has been towards learner-centred courses, which are more likely to meet optimum requirements for learning. The trainer becomes more of a facilitator than a teacher who can provide the answers. For people who have been used to the earlier style, it can be a shock to be faced with a highly participative and experiential course. Instead of being told 'You can effectively manage time by doing the following . . . ', participants might be asked to identify their own time management problems which are then used as a basis for exploring the difficulties and formulating ways of being more effective. Both approaches have their uses. Participants should be told in advance what methods will be used.

5.13.4   In-house or external courses

The term 'in-house' is being used to describe a course consisting of participants from within the organization. It does not have to be on-site and frequently it can be helpful to take the whole group away from daily interruptions and occurrences. Even if 'off-site' it can be on-the-job training. For example, an off-site session attended by senior management to enable them to explore how they work together and set priorities for the next year is very much on-the-job training.

The advantages of running a course in-house are:

- It can be tailored to meet the needs of a particular organization and group of people and made directly relevant to the workplace.
- Achieving an appropriate mix of people and size of group might be easier because control of such factors is held in the organization.
- Dates and length of sessions can be decided by the organization.
- The trainer can be chosen by the organization, whether that person is on the staff or an external provider.
- Development of the organization might be assisted (arising out of a workshop on managing violence and aggression at work could be ideas for changes in existing policies and practices, for example).
- Costs are likely to be lower.

Disadvantages are :

- Participants may feel constrained by the organization and unwilling to explore topics with an open mind.
- The range of experience and knowledge of the group will probably be less than that found on an external course. This will depend on such factors as the length of time people have spent in the organization, experience in other organizations and previous training opportunities.
- Participants may be inhibited. For example, some people find it easier to try out a role play with a group of strangers, though for others it will be more difficult.

The advantages and disadvantages of external courses are in the main the converse of those for in-house courses. They are particularly useful when training is required for only one or two people. When the main objective is to learn new information one person can attend and feed it back to colleagues. This is often referred to as cascade training. However, a participative and experiential approach to training depends on learners having the opportunity to try out skills or have experience of certain situations and hence does not lend itself to cascading.

Careful choice of external courses is likely to be repaid. Matters to be considered are:

- What is the reputation of the organization providing the training?
- What is the reputation of the trainer?
- Do the course description, aims and objectives and programme suggest it will meet the needs of the participant?
- What methods will be used?
- What is the maximum and minimum size of the group?
- At whom is the course targeted?

- Is any pre-course work required?
- Are the date, time and venue suitable?
- What will it cost?

5.13.5 Internal or external trainers

In-house courses might be provided by internal or external trainers. (Here 'internal' is used to mean staff within the department, not other staff from within the organization, such as for example from a central training and development unit.)

Internal trainers have the advantage of knowing the organization, its policies and procedures and probably the people participating. To enable them confidently and competently to undertake the work it is desirable that they have some 'training for trainers'. Opportunities to run courses will enable them to practise skills and further develop their knowledge of group dynamics.

External trainers are likely to be used when no one in-house has the skills, knowledge and experience, or the time, to devote to training. Effective training requires far more than just 'turning up on the day'. More time might be spent in preparing than in working with the group. Furthermore, someone from outside whose primary role is as a training provider and who is not perceived as having an 'axe to grind' in the organization can have greater credibility. This can free the group to work with difficult issues.

If a decision is made to find an external trainer, factors to consider include:

- What is the training and experience of the trainer?
- What experience does s/he have of providing library/information services? Is it important that s/he does?
- What other training work has s/he done?
- What approaches and methods does s/he use? (For example, are they teacher or learner centred?)
- How much does s/he charge? Is it an inclusive fee or are there extras?
- What are the terms in case of cancellation?
- Are they offering a prepared package or is s/he able and willing to tailor a course to the needs of the organization and its staff?
- What is her/his policy on equal opportunities?
- How does s/he provide for her/his own development and what support does s/he have?

5.14 Summary

This chapter set out to:

- describe a range of training methods regularly used in library and information services;
- explore factors to be considered when making decisions about choice of methods.

6 Assessing training

6.1 **Introduction**

It is fortunate that most people think that training is a 'good thing' and can appreciate the arguments in its favour, because assessing what it contributes to a library or information service is not at all easy.

Training texts usually refer to validation and evaluation. The former is about establishing whether training achieves what it sets out to do, and the latter is about examining the total value of training. Checking whether the aims and objectives of a short course have been met might be undertaken by asking participants to complete a feedback form at the end of the day, but trying to evaluate value is much more complex – if achievable at all.

This chapter will begin by looking at when and how training might be assessed, and who is responsible, and then considers the possibility of measuring value/cost-benefit. It assumes that there is a desire to be systematic though questions whether this will prove to be realistic in all situations. Reference should also be made to the guide by Steve Phillips on evaluation.

6.2 When and how to assess training

Assessing training needs to be considered as an integral part of a systematic approach to training, not as an afterthought. However, it can be a difficult and time-consuming task, and the decision to undertake assessment needs to take into account factors such as expense, the importance and frequency of the training, and staff time allocated to the process.

6.2.1 Before training

In Chapter 5 on meeting training needs reference was made to the 'entry behaviour' of the learner. In order to determine at a later stage whether there has been any change in the knowledge, skills or attitude of the trainee, some way of determining her/his existing level, standard or approach must be found.

An appraisal or a performance interview might identify a training need, though it may not provide measures which are sufficiently precise. Other possibilities include tests and questionnaires, which are likely to be time consuming and difficult to prepare. These are potentially useful for establishing existing knowledge – on health and safety procedures, for example, or on census information needed to answer reader enquiries – but probably not for assessing interpersonal skills or other areas of activity for which there are no 'right' answers and in which underlying attitudes significantly affect performance. Such devices may also be useful for facilitating self-assessment by the trainee.

Deciding precise aims and objectives for training at the design stage is crucial for providing a yardstick against which it can be measured. Also, when it comes to detailed planning for the session, time should be built in for feedback so that every effort can be made to meet objectives. During a short course, this could take the form of finding out at the outset what the hopes and concerns of the group are and what they need from the course, and checking later in the session whether or not these requirements are being met.

6.2.2 During training

Being aware of unsolicited feedback, such as lack of engagement with a particular topic or boredom setting in, helps the trainer respond appropriately to the individual or group. Objectives may not be achieved, even when there is potential for them to be met, if such feedback is not noted and acted upon or actively sought out.

A common device used on courses is the action plan. This might be completed during or after the session and provides trainees with a structure for reviewing their learning, for deciding how they will use it in the workplace and for identifying further training needs. It assists the overall assessment of training by encouraging such reflection.

At the end of training, especially on short courses, participants are usually asked to complete a feedback form. A wide range of approaches is used, some focusing on the training environment, catering, skills of the trainer, the expectations of participants and whether these were met; others on what has been learnt and how it will be applied. Those which veer towards the former category and neglect the latter have been described as 'happiness sheets'. They are usually completed when the trainer is still present and the success or otherwise of the day is dominant in the thinking of participants. It is important that there is feedback on all aspects of the training so that improvements can be made to the training and learning reviewed.

6.2.3 After training

There are various possibilities for the subsequent review of learning and how it can be and is applied to the workplace. They include tests, questionnaires, observation of how a particular task/job is being undertaken, discussion with the manager or supervisor and when applicable reconvening the training group. Regarding the last of these, this could take place two weeks after the training and might include talking through the experience of the training and outcomes, including the implications for the organization of the learning which has taken place. A workshop on dealing with readers who are experienced as aggressive might reveal policy issues. The use of tests and questionnaires has been referred to above. Observation could be formal or informal, and to be useful it would need to have provision for feedback on performance to and from the trainee.

Probably the most favoured method of reviewing learning in library and information services is discussion with the trainee's manager/supervisor or the training officer. It provides an opportunity for the manager to show interest in the development of the trainee, help her/him to relate learning to the workplace and job, and identify any further training needs. For it to be effective a review needs to occur soon after the training. It is not satisfactory to await the next appraisal session, which may be many months away.

Longer-term assessment of training might include not only the performance of the individual but also the performance of the organization. What effect has a customer care programme run for everyone in the service had on how library users experience the library? How many complaints are received now, and how does this relate to numbers before the training? Is use of the library on the increase?

However, even if an independent review (conducted before and after training) suggested that user satisfaction was improved, it would be impossible to be sure that this result could be attributed to the training. It could be that staff have been getting stronger messages about the importance of customer care from management.

This section has considered how assessment of training fits into each stage of the cycle. There appears to be an overlap between validation and evaluation. For example, knowledge of the entry behaviour of each trainee will help the trainer meet the aims and objectives of training and provide a basis for subsequent evaluation of its value.

6.3 Who is responsible for assessing training?

One example of how to assess training noted above was for the trainee and her/his manager/supervisor jointly to review learning after a training event. Clearly both have a responsibility: the trainee for considering what s/he has learnt, how it can be applied and identifying further training needs; and the manager for aiding this process. The trainee might also be asked to provide feedback on the event and on how it was organized and facilitated. It is important that trainees are encouraged to take this seriously because only they can be responsible for their own learning. Others can assist.

The manager, by assisting the review of learning, plays a vital role in encouraging staff to value learning opportunities. Managers also contribute to the assessment process by looking out for changes in behaviour, spotting where further training might be needed and intervening when something is inappropriate; for example, poor organization of a training event.

Another person with responsibility for assessment is the training officer. Her/his role is to take an overview of the whole training function. This might include checking out whether transport arrangements for a visit to another library service were satisfactory, obtaining feedback on whether a training event met its stated objectives, facilitating a meeting of participants who had attended an in-house course to review what they had experienced and learnt, and processing feedback forms. A significant task will be to try to measure the benefits of allocating resources to training.

The contribution of the trainer is also important. During training the trainer should constantly be checking out how participants are experiencing the event. This applies as much to teacher-centred as learner-centred training. The lecturer who ignores the fact that half the audience is falling asleep may get through the prepared talk, but will any learning have been facilitated thereby? Other possible roles for the trainer depend on what s/he has been asked to do. For example, an external trainer might be asked to report to the training officer on her/his perception of the general tenor of a training day, further training needs which have been identified, whether s/he felt the training met the aims and objectives and the adequacy of the training room and other facilities.

6.4 Measuring value/cost-benefit

One role of the training officer is to measure the value of training, whether in terms of improved services or of other benefits resulting from allocating resources to it.

As a way of exploring what this involves, consider trying to work out the costs of providing a one-day training course. Obvious costs include hire of a room, printing a publicity leaflet, postage, trainer's fee and expenses, and refreshments. Less easy to calculate are how much time the administrative officer spent on organizing the hire of the room, ensuring that appropriate equipment and so on was available for the course; and how much time the training officer spent on identifying training needs, briefing the trainer, promoting the course, answering queries from potential participants and other associated activities.

Also to be taken into account is the time spent by participants on the course itself, preparing for it and subsequently reviewing their learning; and of managers encouraging attendance and assisting the review process. Just noting some, but by no means all, demands on time for running a one-day course indicates that the financial implications are far more than the obvious costs.

To take it a stage further, let it be assumed that the course is on basic enquiry skills for workers new to library and information services. Having worked out the financial implications, is it possible to establish what value is being added to the organization by allocating resources on this course? One way might be to conduct a survey before and after training to establish levels of service in terms of accuracy and speed. This in itself could demonstrate that the training was worthwhile.

Additionally, can a relationship be shown between spending on training and the benefits to the organization? For example, if no money is spent on the course will the service continue on the same level? Alternatively, can it be demonstrated that the staff who participated now handle more enquiries and require less help from others? Higher productivity could be costed and related to the total course costs, demonstrating the financial advantage of the training.

This is a hypothetical example intended to illustrate some of the potential of measuring value, especially at a time when there is greater emphasis on such approaches. It appears difficult enough to do so for a one-day course, so how would informal and unplanned coaching be considered? One advantage of undertaking such an evaluation would be to strengthen the hand of the training officer in bidding for resources. However, achieving a systematic assessment would be very complex in library and information services, if even possible. Its applications appear to be more obvious in manufacturing, in organizations with large numbers of staff requiring the same training or where financial measures are the primary yardsticks of success.

6.5 Summary

This chapter focused on:

- identifying what assessing training needs means;
- how it fits into the training cycle;
- what methods might be used;
- who is responsible for assessing training needs;
- exploring issues around measuring value and cost-benefit.

7 Who is responsible for training?

7.1 Introduction

The short answer to the question posed above is everyone in an organization, and most people have several responsibilities for training. Besides undertaking their own learning, supervisors may carry out induction training, be part of a staff training group whose primary function is to identify needs and review training, and regularly run a course on handling basic enquiries.

This chapter will look in more detail at the responsibilities of the learner, the trainer, the supervisor/manager, the training officer and administrator, and senior management.

7.2 The learner

As stated before, everyone has responsibility for her/his own learning for no one can learn on behalf of someone else. To realise individual potential for learning, each person may be helped by becoming more aware of how s/he learns and what her/his preferred learning styles are. Greater awareness could lead to grasping opportunities when spotted. For example, the person who realises that s/he tends to be a thinker and likes to reflect on what has been said before saying much, might consider being more spontaneous rather than holding back for fear of making a fool of her/himself. Taking such a risk could lead to appointment to a key committee, or being asked to lead a project, or being asked to write an article, or . . .

Training events provide one opportunity to try out new approaches in a 'safe' environment, in which a person feels able to take risks. Such an approach to learning encourages every activity or part of the day to be regarded as a learning opportunity, though in reality it is unlikely that there would be time to process each activity to find out what had been learnt. However, even the most boring meeting can be analysed privately to determine how it might be conducted differently and what the learner could offer which might bring about change.

Another opportunity is to help others to learn. This does not necessarily mean involvement in formal training events, but could include having the courage to give genuine feedback on performance when asked by a peer, and in so doing to develop interpersonal skills further. This can become a two-way process.

7.3 The trainer

Though an organization may use external trainers, either ones from another part of the organization or independent consultants, possibly everyone except the newest and youngest members of staff is likely to be involved in training others. Most job descriptions include some responsibility for training, though the nature of this might vary considerably. Some will be required mainly to conduct induction training and coaching. Others in addition will run courses, give a lecture or be a mentor. While some library and information services have a training officer, few have full-time trainers. Even if they did, it would not affect the desirability of everyone contributing to training.

As with any task it will be important for each person undertaking training to develop the relevant skills and knowledge. Depending on what training is involved, examples include interpersonal skills, how to set up an overhead projector, presentation skills, knowledge and experience of working with groups, using a flip chart, deciding the most appropriate layout of a training room for a particular course, and an overview of the training cycle.

7.4 The manager/supervisor

A key task of managers and supervisors is to contribute actively to all aspects of the training cycle. Without such an example from the manager or supervisor, training will be regarded as less significant within the organization. They will need to be seen to be concerned with their own learning as well as that of others; otherwise confused messages about the importance of learning will be sent out. The manager who decrees that training is 'a good thing' and that everyone in her/his department, except her/himself, will go on customer care training may well undermine the outcome.

7.5 The training officer

Many library and information services have a training officer whose job it is to concentrate on the training function in the organization. S/he may have a training/personnel background and qualifications or may come to this post following experience as a library and information service provider. Other organizations will require this role to be performed as part of a wider range of duties. Often the training officer will be the person with overall responsibility for personnel matters. Sometimes the budget and main responsibility for training within the whole organization is vested with a centralized training and development department.

The size of the library and information service may be a determining factor. There is no 'right' way of allocating this responsibility and the outcome is likely to depend on the abilities of the individual and the commitment to training within the organization. Access to and influence on key decision makers may be aided if the training officer is a member of this group. Such influence is important to secure commitment and resources to a systematic approach to training.

The emphasis of the training officer's duties will vary though all might expect to contribute to all aspects of the training cycle. For example, some might do little or no direct training, others might spend a significant proportion of their time running courses. Some may have to do all or much of the organization of training, while others may have administrative support to assist in this part of the process. Control of the training budget is likely to be an issue. If it is the manager's concern, will s/he take her/his responsibility for training more seriously and the training officer perceive her/his role to be undermined? Or if it is the training officer's concern, will training be regarded by managers as someone else's responsibility and hence be marginalized?

A significant role of the training officer is to keep in touch with developments in the field. This might involve being part of a training group attended by representatives from other organizations to pool knowledge and experience, reading journals, and identifying suitable external trainers, and liaising with the central training team within the organization.

7.6 Administrative officer

The contribution of the administrative officer can greatly enhance the training function. The next chapter looks in more detail at the range of tasks to be performed.

7.7 Senior management

In addition to relevant responsibilities listed above, the key role of senior managers will be to indicate their own commitment to training and to secure that of their organization. This may be demonstrated in many ways, though probably obtaining and allocating resources is the most important. For example, this could include negotiating with the parent body that the library will open an hour later once a week to enable training to take place, or ensuring that any reviews of staffing levels have built in consideration of how much time might appropriately be allowed for training. The Library Association[1] recommends allowing between 28 and 42 hours a year for continuing professional development activities. These figures are intended as a guide and are based on existing good practice (best practice exceeds that figure).

7.8 Influencing providers

It is important for all library and information staff, and not just the training officer, to be outward looking. For example, another role of senior managers, one not exclusively theirs, is to influence external providers to ensure satisfactory provision is made to meet the needs of their organization. This might include liaising with professional bodies, academic institutions and other training providers. An existing first-degree course leading to a professional qualification for librarians might be found to be inadequate in some areas. Stating which of the contents prove their worth, which do not and which are perceived to be missing will help the university providing the course, and could lead to a better match between what is needed and what is provided.

7.9 Co-operative working

Many library and information services join up with others to provide training, to share information and act as an informal support group for the training officers. In some cases it might be the only way of providing cost- and time-effective training. An example is when several college libraries with relatively small numbers of staff group together to provide a training course for their staff rather than sending them one by one to an external course in another part of the country.

7.10 New approaches

This guide has emphasized the value of a systematic approach to training.

One warning about this is that sometimes it is more important to seize the opportunity when it arises than to wait for the perfectly planned session – for example, to take the chance afforded by a problem that is happening now to work out how to tackle it. To conclude this chapter, a brief look is taken at two exciting current concepts which may provide ways of further enhancing the training and development of staff.

7.10.1 Self-managed learning

Throughout this guide consideration has been given to providing the best conditions for learning to take place. In recent years the concept of self-managed learning which appears to meet these conditions, has been developed. Features include individuals taking responsibility for designing their own learning, in conjunction with a tutor or line manager and other learners, so that it suits their experience and learning needs and the requirements of the organization. Individuals are encouraged to learn for themselves rather than being taught ideas which might soon be out of date. One model is for the learner to draw up a learning contract with her/his line manager and organization, and to plan and direct her/his own programme, supported by attendance at an action learning set. Managing a library project or developing a strategic plan could be the basis of the contract.[23]

7.10.2 The learning organization

The other prevalent concept is the desirability of moving towards a learning organization. On one level it has been suggested that any organization which survives for a reasonable time is a learning organization. However, this is making a narrow interpretation of the idea. Themes applied to the term include continual transformation of the organization linked to the development of all its members so that change is achieved relatively gradually and smoothly, rather than through major crises from time to time. Its attainment requires library and information workers to be skilled learners and calls for a work environment, which enhances rather than inhibits learning.[4]

It seems to the author that this is a worthwhile goal. The systematic approach described throughout underpins such an objective. This could be reinforced by working towards national standards leading to an award such as the *Investors in people* kite mark. To reach out to become a learning organization at its strongest is a major undertaking and would require all members of the organization to embrace the idea of continuous learning and work towards an environment which enhances learning.

7.11 Summary

This chapter set out to:

- describe the training responsibilities of each person in the organization;
- demonstrate the need to influence and be aware of developments beyond the library and information service;
- consider the two relatively recent concepts of self-managed learning and the learning organization.

8 Organization and administration of training

8.1 Introduction

A systematic approach to training requires good organization and administration. When it is in place all aspects of the training cycle are likely to proceed smoothly. Without it, training events can be undermined even by small happenings such as coffee not arriving at the promised time. This chapter focuses on translating training plans into programmes, budgets, resources, monitoring and equal opportunities, and on the administration which needs to be attended to before, during and after each training event.

8.2 Training plans and programmes

Producing a training plan enables clarification of which identified training needs will be met in any given period, usually a financial year. A plan might set out what training will be provided, how it will meet needs, how it will be undertaken, what the expected outcome will be and the desired time scale. For example, one entry might note that 25 library assistants and their supervisors require knowledge and practice using a replacement computer issue system which will enable them to operate it immediately after it is installed in three months' time. The proposed method of training is a one-day off-the-job course provided by the computer company supplying the new equipment followed by short individual practice sessions, each learner being provided with a terminal set up to simulate how the new system will function, and a work book.

This needs to be translated into a programme which will set out when and for whom the training is to be provided. Such a programme must take local conditions into account . If it has been decided that the main priority is to ensure the smooth introduction of the computer issue system, it will be important that staff who need to be trained are kept clear of other commitments if they are likely to clash. Some times of the year may be ruled out for some types of training. For example, for a university library the start of the new academic year is not usually a good time for in-house short courses requiring the attendance of a group of people to make them viable.

Successful planning of training events is not something which can be done in isolation. The training officer needs to be aware of overall priorities and plans and to be prepared to explain and negotiate the time required by staff to undertake training, otherwise training events are likely to be sidelined because staff feel it is more important to do their day-to-day work. In the long term this is likely to be to the detriment of the organization.

One matter to be considered is whether or not it is appropriate to plan for the whole year. When change is rapid, training needs may emerge which had not been envisaged, yet it is considered vital that they are met. No planning is likely to lead to little training happening, whereas if the total training budget is allocated at the beginning of the financial year a degree of flexibility is lost.

8.3 Budgeting

Training officers may have to maintain detailed budgets and monitor expenditure, though this is likely to depend on the accounting system used in the organization. In any case it will be helpful to build up a picture of how the training budget is being used to enable analysis of spending and assist future planning; for example, how much per head is the norm for attendance on an external short course, what is spent on distance learning and how much does it cost per person, how much is spent on travel or paying overtime to cover for absences on training, what is the break-even point for hiring an external trainer rather than sending some staff on a course, and how much does it cost to hire a suitable room for an event?

8.4 Resources

Part of the budget will be spent on providing appropriate resources to support training. These might range from keeping sufficient supplies of flip chart paper and pens to equipping and maintaining a training room with appropriate computer terminals. Given the high use of information technology in library and information services, equipment to support training may be expensive and require constant updating. Video recorders and players, television, audio cassette players, overhead projectors and screens and the flip chart are all commonly used training aids.

Additionally, appropriate equipment will be needed to support the organization and administration of training. Minimum requirements will include word-processing and photocopying facilities. Other aids might be appropriate software packages for organizing training and desktop publishing.

Whether these resources are available for the exclusive use of the training function or whether they are shared with other groups of staff will depend to a large extent on the size of the library and information service. In many organizations, and particularly the smaller ones, expensive equipment is likely to be held centrally and access to it will have to be negotiated. This can be an efficient use of resources but may involve complex planning and organization. Much time can be spent on co-ordination – for example, checking the availability of the participants and the trainer(s), booking a room and catering, getting hand-outs produced on time, ordering a training video and arranging with a central store for a television and video player to be set up.

The other main resource is the training officer, trainers and administrative staff. Besides undertaking all the tasks so far described in this chapter and elsewhere, their attitude to training will have an immense significance on outcomes. For example, a senior library assistant may seek the opportunity to check out her/his understanding of how a visit to another library might help her/him – what in particular can be learnt from what is happening on the site to be visited? How such an interaction is handled will to some degree affect learning, because it contributes to the overall impression staff will form of training and its importance in the organization.

Efficient organization and administration will cut out many requests for further information. For example, a map showing the training venue accompanied by a description of how to get there will stop most people from ringing up to request this information.

8.5 Monitoring

Many aspects of monitoring have already been referred to, such as keeping a check on the budget and equipment. A significant area not yet mentioned is who the training is for. Frequently, take-up of training, other than induction and that resulting from overall legal or policy changes, is restricted to a relatively small group of senior staff and self-selectors, that is, the people who ask for training. This is not likely to be in the best interests of the organization. If the organization is trying to promote training and learning, restriction of it will send out contradictory messages. Nor does it encourage equal opportunities.

It is recognized that access to training plays a significant part in enabling staff to develop their potential and hence prepare them for job changes and/or promotion. Monitoring take-up of training is a step towards reviewing who has access to training. This might be achieved by categorizing trainees; for example, by grade, sex, ethnicity, whether able-bodied or disabled or whether full- or part-time. Over a period of time patterns will emerge which can be reviewed, and necessary changes implemented. For example, if it emerges that staff who use a wheelchair are not represented in the figures, further investigation may reveal that locations used were not wheelchair accessible. If few part-time staff feature, it may emerge that managers regard them differently, saying, 'They're only in it for pin money; so as long as they can do their job it's not worth sending them on a management development course.'

Such monitoring is only likely to cover formal and planned training. For example, it would not reveal that a specific manager was whole-heartedly encouraging and coaching the full-time members of staff and largely ignoring the needs of part-timers.

8.6 Equal opportunities

Monitoring take-up of training is one aspect of applying equal opportunity policies. It is vital that when all parts of the training cycle are implemented, equal opportunities are held in focus; for example, at the stage of identifying training needs by noting that female staff and staff from ethnic minorities seek management training designed specifically for them. When meeting needs, this might involve rejecting a video because it stereotypes the roles of black people, ensuring hand-outs do not use sexist language or contain offensive graphics, carefully weighing up a psychological test because it is based on norms for white male managers or challenging course participants who use racist language. An example of factors for consideration when assessing training is that of measuring performance before and after a training event to determine what and whose standards are being met. Are they based more on style than performance?

Any organization which sets out to be a learning organization will need to embrace equal opportunities policies, for only then will all its members feel that they can make a full contribution.

8.7 Administration

Given the range of training events which might be used, it is difficult to identify all the matters which must be thought about before, during and after each event. For example, a visit to another organization might necessitate the following: booking a minibus, identifying a driver, checking her/his licence and making appropriate insurance provision; drawing up a list of people going on the visit; making arrangements with the other organization about parking, arrival and departure times; establishing who is the contact and who will be available on the day; explaining arrangements to participants; issuing, receiving and processing forms used to claim lunch expenses; afterwards finding out about and recording attendance; processing the invoice from the minibus hire firm. For what is a relatively simple training event there is much administration to be undertaken.

8.8 Summary

This chapter focused on:

- translating training plans into programmes;
- budgeting;
- obtaining and managing resources for training;
- monitoring take-up of training;
- training and the implementation of equal opportunities policies;
- administration of training.

⑨ Summary

This guide has advocated a systematic approach to the management of training and staff development, underpinned by the regular use of the training cycle: identifying and meeting training needs; and assessing the outcome. The cycle can also be used to react to unexpected performance problems or plan for specific organizational changes. The systematic approach is applicable to all sizes of library and information service.

The phrases 'systematic approach' and 'training cycle' might suggest a cold and mechanical process. The reality is different. On one level, training is managed by people for people and all those engaged in the management of training require appropriate interpersonal and 'change agent' skills. At another level, it is important to be aware of the context in which training is being managed and to look to the future, for there is no point in training staff to provide yesterday's services.

An important aspect of managing training is attention to detail. A wrongly spelt name might suggest a lack of respect for the trainee; the choice of terms mght convey unintended messages. In the library and information world the following words are laiden with meaning: consumer, reader, user, client, customer.

Rapid change raises other issues. For the manager of training and staff development, reconciling a systematic approach with a flexible and rapid response may prove to be difficult.

One change being encouraged within the library and information world is for staff to assume responsibility, along with employers and professional organizations, for their own continuing development. This is likely to shift the emphasis away from 'being taught' to individual responsibility for learning. Rather than waiting to be told the 'right' solution, the active learner will search out answers to her/his questions. In line with such a development, the primary role of the training manager might be fulfilled, by focusing on helping staff become skilled learners and influencing their service towards providing an environment which enables and encourages learning.

References

Chapter 5
1   Northern Training Group and SCET, *Co-operative training, open learning and public library staffs: Public library development incentive scheme (PLDIS): Interim report*, November 1992, Glasgow, SCET, 1992.
    (The first open learning module *Financial management for librarians: managing resources* was published December 1993. Enhancing services for disabled library users was published in May 1994 and a module on dealing with difficult situations is intended for publication in 1994.

Chapter 7
1   The Library Association, *Your personal profile: the framework for continuing professional development*, The Library Association, 1992.
2   Corrall, S., 'Self managed learning: the key to professional and personal development' in Foreman, L. (ed.), *Developing professionals in information work: personal and organisational growth in libraries*, (Circle of State Librarians), London, HMSO, 1992.
3   Hurley, B. and Cunningham, I., 'Imbibing a new way of learning', *Personnel management*, **25** (3), 1993, 42–5.
4   Burgoyne, J., 'Creating a learning organisation', *RSA journal*, **140** (4), 1992, 321–32.

Selective bibliography

Burgoyne, J., 'Creating a learning organisation', *RSA journal*, **140** (4), 1992, 321–32.

Corrall, S., 'Self managed learning: the key to professional and personal development' in Foreman, L. (ed.), *Developing professionals in information work: personal and organisational growth in libraries*, (Circle of State Librarians), London, HMSO, 1992.

Fisher, B., *Mentoring*, London, Library Association Publishing, 1994.

Handy, C., *The age of unreason*, London, Hutchinson, 1989.

Honey, P., 'The learning organisation simplified', *Training and development*, **9** (7), 1991, 30–3.

Honey, P. and Mumford, A., *The manual of learning styles*, 3rd edn., Maidenhead, Peter Honey, 1992.

Honey, P. and Mumford, A., *Using your learning styles*, 2nd edn., Maidenhead, Peter Honey, 1986.

Hunt, C., 'Library staff development consultancy: a means to achieve a better library', *Personnel training and education: a journal for library and information workers*, **8** (1), 1991, 3–7.

Hurley, B. and Cunningham, I., 'Imbibing a new way of learning', *Personnel management*, **25** (3), 1993, 42–5.

Kolb, D., *Experiential learning*, Prentice Hall, 1985.

The Library Association, *The framework for continuing professional development: your personal profile*, London, The Library Association, 1992.

Mumford, A., 'How managers can become developers', *Personnel management*, **25** (6), 1993, 42–5.

Nicholson, H., 'Staff development: getting it done', *Personnel training and education: a journal for library and education workers*, **8** (3), 1991, 65–8.

Noon, P., 'Starting from scratch: developing a staff training and development programme in an academic library', *Personnel training and education: a journal for library and information workers*, **9** (3), 1992, 65–71.

Northern Training Group and SCET, *Co-operative training, open learning and public library staffs: Public library development incentive scheme (PLDIS): Interim report*, November 1992, Glasgow, SCET, 1992.

Phillips, K. and Fraser, T., *The management of interpersonal skills training*, Aldershot, Gower, 1982.

Phillips, S., *Evaluation*, Library Association Publishing, London, 1993.

Prytherch, R. (ed.), *Handbook of library training practice 1*, Aldershot, Gower, 1986.

Prytherch, R. (ed.), *Handbook of library training practice 2*, Aldershot, Gower, 1991.

Robinson, K., *A handbook of training management*, 2nd edn., London, Kogan Page, 1988.

Rogers, J., *Adults learning*, 3rd edn., Milton Keynes, Open University Press, 1989.

Slater, M., *Investment in training: a quick, qualitative conspection in the library–information field*, (British Library R&D report 6048), British Library Research and Development Department, 1991.

Staff Development Committee, Personnel Administration Section, Library Administration and Management Association, American Library Association, *Staff development: a practical guide*, 2nd edn., Chicago, American Library Association, 1992.

Taylor, A., *Continuing professional development for library and information science staff in the south west: report for the year October 1990–September 1991*, Bath, A. B. Taylor, 1991.

Williamson, M., *Training needs analysis*, London, Library Association Publishing, 1993.

Working Party on Training, *Training in libraries*, London, The Library Association, 1977.

Appendix
Sample working documents

1 Aston University Library & Information Services: Staff development and training policy statement (Revised version November 1993).
2 East Sussex County Library Service: Training policy.
3 University of Nottingham, University Library: Policy on training and staff development (November 1992).
4 Aston University Library & Information Services: Checklists for identifying development and training needs (Revised version 1993).
5 East Sussex County Library Service: Human Resource Development, 1992–3: Report to Departmental Management Team (March 1993).
6 Hertfordshire Libraries Arts & Information: Library Assistants' Development Programme (extract) (1993).
7 June Whetherly and University of Huddersfield: Course on effective training designed and run for the University of Huddersfield: Aim and objectives, programme and extract from trainer's plan (November 1993).
8 University of West of England Library Service: Policy document 1993 (extract) (December 1992).
9 East Sussex County Library Service: Training events checklist.
10 University of Nottingham Library: Application to attend external course/conference/visit (September 1992).

Acknowledgements
Due acknowledgement is given to all the individuals and organizations whose working documents are reproduced here.

Example 1

ASTON UNIVERSITY
LIBRARY & INFORMATION SERVICES

STAFF DEVELOPMENT AND TRAINING
Policy Statement

Introduction

The University has recently agreed the purpose of its staff development process as,

> "to assist and encourage all staff to develop their skills and knowledge and thus enhance their contribution to the University".

The Library & Information Services (LIS) is fully committed to the above statement, and has already stated its position on staff development in the LIS Strategic Plan, describing its style of provision as characterised by,

> "full commitment to a continuing programme of staff development at all levels, to ensure that individuals and teams can contribute with maximum effect to the fulfilment of LIS objectives and develop their own potential".

In accordance with the above, LIS sees staff development and training both as a *continuous process* and as a *shared responsibility* between the individual and the organisation. It acknowledges that staff are the department's most important resource and that its human resources strategy must be integrated with the overall LIS strategy. To this end, within a *supportive environment* , LIS undertakes to:

- translate departmental objectives and related plans into complementary programmes for the development of staff at all levels throughout the department;
- encourage all staff to engage in individual programmes of continuous self-development, and to regard work tasks as offering potential for self-development;
- work jointly with individuals to identify career options open to them and plan appropriate tailored programmes of functional and management development.

A range of development and training methods will be employed (including both on-the-job and off-the-job activities) but there will be an emphasis on work-based learning tailored to particular needs, reflecting a general trend in this direction and a widespread view that it produces better results, enabling more effective translation of skills and knowledge back to the operational environment.

Thus LIS sees its responsibilities as extending beyond immediate job needs and is prepared to support the development of skills and knowledge relevant to individuals' future careers, irrespective of whether they may be at Aston or elsewhere. LIS will work in partnership with the University's Staff Development Office in furtherance of the above, and together they will make the necessary budgetary provision to ensure that all staff have the chance to achieve their full potential. At the same time the organisation expects individuals to take advantage of learning opportunities available, to evaluate what they have learned and to share this with colleagues. All staff will be encouraged to take part in professional activities at regional and national levels and to acquire appropriate membership qualifications (eg Associateship/Fellowship of the Library Association, Corporate Membership of the Institute of Information Scientists). The level of financial and other support provided will be determined by institutional policies and priorities, and in some cases may take the form of partial not full support (eg BTEC courses).

Example 1 continued

Roles and responsibilities

The **DIRECTOR OF LIS** is responsible for ensuring the integration of the department's human resources strategy with the department's overall strategy, and for creating a supportive environment conducive to learning and development.

In addition to her specific line management responsibilities, she has a general responsibility to lead, guide and facilitate the career management and development of all LIS senior staff.

The **HEAD OF MANAGEMENT SERVICES** acts as the department's Staff Development and Training Officer.

She is responsible for formulating and implementing strategic and operational plans for human resources management, which includes conducting an annual development and training needs analysis for the department (in conjunction with line managers) and liaising with the Staff Development Office; liaising with counterparts in other libraries, eg through the West Midlands Regional Library System Training Officers Group; providing information and advice to line managers; managing the department's development and training budget; and monitoring and evaluating progress against objectives.

In addition to her specific line management responsibilities, she has a general responsibility to lead, guide and facilitate the career management and development of the support staff cadre.

LINE MANAGERS are responsible for ensuring the development of relevant skills and knowledge by their staff, to enable them to improve performance and achieve their full potential.

They have a duty to monitor performance, to diagnose both short-term and longer term development and training needs, to identify and create learning opportunities, to provide encouragement and support, to give and receive feedback, to counsel and coach staff, and to evaluate progress against learning objectives.

They have a specific formal responsibility to discuss training and development needs in the context of the annual staff appraisal cycle, but this must be supplemented by regular informal discussions throughout the year.

ALL STAFF (including the above) are responsible for clarifying their own learning and career goals within the framework established by the department and agreeing specific objectives with their line managers.

In addition, they have a responsibility to evaluate what they have learned and to share their learning with colleagues. Ideally, this applies to all learning experiences, and not simply to attendance at formal events when support is conditional on the completion of an evaluation form.

The **STAFF DEVELOPMENT OFFICE** is responsible for formulating and implementing strategic and operational plans for the University as a whole.

Its roles encompass provision of on-site courses on general management topics and in personal skills, including IT training, and also development and provision of tailored workshops to meet specific departmental needs; dissemination of information on courses organised by the CVCP Universities' Staff Development Unit, by the Midland Universities' Support Staff Training and Development Group (MUSSTAD) and by other higher education institutions; and financial support for the above courses, selective support for other expensive courses, and partial support for courses leading to qualifications (eg BTEC, City & Guilds, DMS).

revised November 1993

Example 2

East Sussex County Library Service

Training Policy

Overall Purpose

Where possible to provide facilities. financial support, advice and opportunities to enable employee to acquire the attitudes, skills and knowledge needed to perform effectively the duties and tasks for which they are employed and to develop their potential to meet the future human resource needs of the service.

Training Aims

(1)   That every Manager and Supervisor understands and is assisted to meet his or her responsibility for the training and development of employees under his or her control.

(2)   That training needs of all employees are met in the most effective way by:-
   (i)   practical training given within the Authority; or,
   (ii)   training provided outside the Authority; with
   (iii)   emphasis being placed on the development of training provided within the Authority;
   (iv)   training evaluation procedures being instituted; and
   (v)   comprehensive training records being maintained.

Co-ordination of training

The Training Officer will have an overall co-ordinating role in training. S/he will undertake an advisory function for all training matters and will maintain contact with officers of the County Council's Training Group who may give advice and/or practical support in certain cases.

The role of the Manager/Supervisor

The task of management is to ensure the best possible use of all resources to meet the objectives of the organisation. People are our greatest resource and therefore their effective contribution is of paramount importance. The training and development of staff is the responsibility of the manager or supervisor. The Training Officer cannot take over these responsibilities but should give assistant and active support as necessary.

Training should not be an end in itself, it must be seen to be effective in terms of overall objectives. There is a need to ensure that employees undergoing training see its relevance to their present jobs and career prospects. Managers and supervisors must ensure, therefore that the new skills and knowledge acquired can be used in the workplace. This may well require flexibility to allow for changed work methods, techniques and attitudes. training is no longer just the passing on of old skills to new people, it is learning to apply new skills to existing or new situations.

Example 3

UNIVERSITY OF NOTTINGHAM

UNIVERSITY LIBRARY

POLICY ON TRAINING AND STAFF DEVELOPMENT

POLICY STATEMENT

It is the policy of the Library to ensure that positive and continuous support and encouragement are given to all staff in respect of their training and staff development so that they acquire the skills necessary both for the furtherance of their careers and for the delivery of the best possible service to all library users.

AIMS

1. To provide basic training to enable all library staff to carry out their work as effectively and efficiently as possible.

2. To encourage a wide knowledge and understanding of the teaching and research work of the University and other funding bodies and to promote an awareness of the role of the library in support of that work.

3. To ensure that staff are kept up-to-date with technological change and innovation.

4. To encourage awareness of new developments and changing concepts in the library and information world.

5. To encourage all staff to develop good interpersonal and communication skills to that they are able to co-operate effectively with colleagues and to relate well to the great variety of library users.

6. To encourage long-term career development of all staff on all grades.

7. To ensure that all newly qualified librarians gain the skills and experience necessary to achieve the Library Association Chartership.

8. To provide training which ensures compliance with Health and Safety legislation.

9. To promote awareness of the services and the resources available in each of the University's libraries.

10. To encourage exchange visits with the local libraries and information centres.

11. To encourage an awareness of the publishing industry.

12. To encourage support staff to take advantage of vocational training opportunities.

13. To ensure regular review and evaluation of the above policy.

6.11.92

Example 4

ASTON UNIVERSITY
LIBRARY & INFORMATION SERVICES

Checklists for identifying development and training needs

MANAGING THE BUSINESS

FINANCIAL MANAGEMENT/
MANAGEMENT ACCOUNTING

Cost centre management and
budgetary control
Costing activities/services
Preparing estimates/budget bids
Monitoring commitment and
expenditure
Interpreting financial reports
Investment appraisal
Performance measurement/indicators
Resource allocation within LIS
University finance system
Finance in Higher Education
Institutions

STRATEGIC PLANNING AND
MANAGEMENT

Environmental scanning
Situation analysis
Vision and mission
Objectives and goals
Key result areas/
critical success factors
Strategies and action plans
Communication and implementation
Operational planning
Monitoring and evaluation
Planning and budgeting cycle

MARKETING

Customer care
Market research
Service/product portfolio
Product planning and development
Delivery/distribution channels
Charging and pricing policies
Promotional literature
Advertising/publicity
Survey methods
Public relations

INFORMATION SYSTEMS

CD-ROM products
Online services
Local databases
Library housekeeping
- acquisitions/serials and
  bibliographic records
- circulation
- ILL
- OPAC
Networked services
(LIS/ACCENT/JANET)
Management information systems

ORGANISATIONAL BEHAVIOUR

National higher education policy (eg
HEFC, CVCP, HE Quality Council)
Institutional history
Faculty and departmental organisation
Committee structure
Decision-making processes
Industrial relations/Trade Unions
Health and safety at work
Culture
Professional ethics
Total Quality Management

PROFESSIONAL UPDATING

Copyright: photocopying and
downloading/electrocopying
Data protection and customer records
Disaster preparedness
Information sources

ANY OTHER TOPICS

....
....
....

1

Example 4   continued

ASTON UNIVERSITY
LIBRARY & INFORMATION SERVICES

Checklists for identifying development and training needs

MANAGING OTHERS

Leadership/supervisory styles

Communication
Listening skills
Negotiation
Delegation
Motivation

Team building
Handling conflict
Chairing meetings
Facilitation of groups
Training and instruction

Staff appraisal
Setting objectives
Monitoring performance
Giving and receiving feedback
Diagnosing development
 and training needs
Coaching/mentoring
Counselling

Disciplinary procedures

Performance-related pay

Recruitment procedures
- job descriptions and
  person specifications
- selection interviewing

Employment contracts

Equal opportunities

Data protection and personnel records

ANY OTHER TOPICS

....
....
....
....

MANAGING YOURSELF

Attending meetings,
 presenting papers,
 taking minutes

Public speaking

Filing systems

Telephone techniques
Time (and stress) management

Problem solving
Project management

Reading skills
Research methods and
 statistical techniques
Writing letters,
 memoranda,
 reports

OFFICE AUTOMATION/PERSONAL
PRODUCTIVITY TOOLS

Keyboard skills
Mac awareness
Electronic mail
Databases
Graphics

Word processing (eg Word)
Spreadsheets (eg Excel)
Bibliographic management
(eg ProCite)
Project management
Desk-top publishing

....
....
....
....

2

Example 4   continued

ASTON UNIVERSITY
LIBRARY & INFORMATION SERVICES

Checklists for identifying development and training needs

INDUCTION

UNIVERSITY
(Main Building)

Conditions of service
(Personnel Services)

Staff identity card
(Audio Visual & Photographic
Services)

LIS

Tour of LIS
(Line manager)

Flexitime + Paging system
(Head of Management Services)

Health & Safety + Copyright
(Head of Library Services)

Strategic priorities
(Director)

Organisational structure
(Head of Management Services)

LIBRARY SERVICES DIVISION

Acquisitions
(Acquisitions Manager)

Bibliographic Records
(Bibliographic Records Manager)

Circulation
(Document Supply Manager)

Counter services
(Senior Library Assistant,
Document Supply)

Interlibrary Loans
(Senior Library Assistant,
ILL)

INFORMATION SERVICES DIVISION

Information Services
(Head of Information Services)

MANAGEMENT SERVICES

Office services
(Office Manager/Clerical Assistant)

Planning
(Planning Officer)

Professional Development Report
(Head of Management Services)

Total Quality Management
(Head of Management Services)

SYSTEMS

Systems & Networks
(Head of Systems/Computer Officer)

Mac awareness,
Introduction to Word,
Introduction to Excel
(Staff Development)

SPECIFIC JOB-RELATED NEEDS
(including courses, visits, etc)

Tour of section/division
(Line manager)

....
....
....
....

Induction review
(Line manager)

3

Example 5

Human Resource Development, 1992-3

Report to Departmental Management Team – 9 March 1993

1. 1992/3

1.1 By the end of the financial year:-
823 people will have attended 158 training events (948 days training).
This excludes locally organised events and on-the-job training.
For comparison with previous years see Appendix A.

1.2 6 people successfully completed their BTEC course in June 1992 and six
more began Year 1 in September 1992. 10 have attained the LIAC; 4 more
are working to complete their modules.

1.3 Four Team Librarians have begun modules in 1992/3 these will be completed
in 1993/4.

1.4 All this will have been achieved at an estimated cost of £26,518, an
overspend of £2,218. The overspend is mainly due to additional demand for
team development and recruitment and selection training.

2 1993/4 – budget £19,000 (equivalent to £45 a head)

2.1 Committed expenditure
Qualification courses underway + courses already
booked.   £3,100

2.2 Functional bids
For details see Appendix C.   **£7,760**

These bids do not take into account all the TNA requests from specialist
staff (conferences/LA courses, etc). Bids for these are included in "TNA
Requests" under Professional development.

2.3 **TNA Requests**
For details see Appendix C.   **£29,495**

2.3.1 Senior/Middle management development training programmes will be
provided as part of the Service Level Agreement with the County Personnel
Department.

2.4 Grand total needed to meet all expressed needs =   **£40,395!**

3 Possible ways forward.

3.1 Functional training
From my attendance at a Public Services meeting in November last year, I
believe that most function heads would be prepared to commit part of their
budget to functional training. I propose that they are asked to either, set
aside a set sum each, say £1,000, or guarantee to underwrite the major in-

Example 5 **continued**

house events.

Recommendation: that functional heads be asked to contribute to the cost of functional training. (£1,000 each?)

** **Not agreed. Recommendation carried forward to Policy Advisory Team that training expenses be paid from area budgets – AGREED by PAT.**

3.2 Central training programme requests

3.2.1 In 1992/3 Library Service staff took a total of 66 places on County Council courses, 31 of these were centrally funded.
These courses are used:
   a) when in-house expertise is not available;
   b) when there are too few nominations to make an in-house course viable.
Waiting lists are getting longer as the range of courses available increases and staff recognise the value of attending these courses.

3.2.2 **Recommendation:** that **£2,500** be allocated to these courses

** **AGREED**

3.3 In-house courses
The highest priority continues to be to provide staff with the appropriate skills and knowledge to enable them to provide core services to our users. The cost of external courses has continued to rise steadily despite the recession so that the average daily cost of external courses is now £120. Obviously the most effective use of the training budget will be to continue to organise in house events, buying in consultants where appropriate and using our premises wherever possible. In this way a days training averages around £25.

3.3.1 **Recommendation:** that the in-house programme of skills development be continued as follows:-

	£
Customer care **x 1**	200
Dealing with difficult situations **x 2**	1,800
Effective supervision **x 1**	800
Interpersonal communication skills **x 1**	400
Recruitment and selection **x 1**	200
TNA/Counselling skills **x 1**	200
Trainer skills **x 1**	400
A total of:	**£4,000**

** **AGREED**

Example 5 | **continued**

3.4 <u>Health and Safety</u>

3.4.1 **Recommendation:** to continue to work towards training in aspects of health and safety awareness for all staff and to for adequate first aid cover in all service points, by providing the following:

Fire protection (½ day) x 8 (locally based)	400
Safety policy workshops x 3 (½ day)	350
Lifting and handling training (assessors and staff)	200
First Aid – qualification x 6	780
– recertification x 8	640
– Appointed persons courses x 10	100
– local "emergency" courses x 3	100

A total of: **£2,570**

** **AGREED**

3.5 <u>Awareness visits, etc</u>

These visits have more than proved their worth in that staff are more fully informed on services available outside their own workplace. Communication is enhanced and they are able to assist users more readily.

3.5.1 **Recommendation:** that the programme of services awareness visits be continued as in 1992/3.

HQ "Open days" x 8	400
LGU / Record Office visits x 8	400
Store "open day"	100
MIU "shadow" visits x 6	180

A total of: **£1080**

** **AGREED**

3.5.2 **Recommendation:** that expenses arising from all other visits, i.e. those arranged within areas or participation in SASLIC, Aslib, etc visits be paid for either from local funds or by the participants.

3.6 <u>Qualification training</u>

3.6.1 <u>BTEC</u> - there will be no new starts this year. Year 2 costs have been included in committed expenditure.

3.6.2 <u>LIAC</u> – this is an excellent all round introduction to library and information work. The local college course is greatly enjoyed by its participants and the open learning course is excellent for those with the self discipline for private study. There is a lot of interest in the course, not only as a route to career progression but as a way of finding out about the wider world of library and information.

Example 5 continued

The course costs an average of £320 at Lewes Tertiary College and £270 by open learning.

Recommendation: that we support 6 places at Lewes Tertiary College and 4 open learning places.   Total cost **£3,540**

**   **AGREED**

3.7   Foreign language training
Will continue to be offered as part of the County Personnel Department SLA.

3.8   Professional Development Courses
There are many specialist areas of our work where it would not be viable to organise our own events.   It is important that these staff have the opportunity to attend courses/conferences where they can meet and exchange ideas and knowledge with people from other organisations working in similar fields.

3.8.1   **Recommendation:** that **£2,500** be allocated to these courses.

**   **AGREED**

4   **Analysis of recommendations**

		£
3.2	Central training programme	2,500
3.3	In house courses	4,000
3.4	Health and safety	2,570
3.5	Awareness visits	930
3.6	LIAC	3,540
3.8	Professional Development	2,500
Sub total		**16,040**
Committed expenditure		3,100
Total		**19,140**

As I have rounded up all the individual figures, I am confident that the actual total could be reduced to £19,000.

Christine Millum
5 March 1993

Example 6

LIBRARY ASSISTANTS' DEVELOPMENT PROGRAMME (LADP)

Introduction

The LADP is open to all staff employed as Library Assistants in HLAI. It aims to build on the induction process by providing:

*   a framework for staff to develop the skills, knowledge and understanding required to provide an effective Library and Information Service in Hertfordshire

*   opportunities for self-development and experience which could lead to career progression

*   a flexible staffing resource for HLAI, and opportunities for local managers to develop and utilise individual expertise and skills creatively and effectively

*   a full and accurate record of an individual's development and training activities and opportunities, with reference to work assessment where appropriate and possible.

Key elements of the LADP are:

i. **choice** - the decision as to whether to participate in the LADP rests with the individual; however, managers will be expected to encourage their staff to do so, particularly as far as Stage II which covers the fundamental range of skills and knowledge required for working effectively as part of the team of staff in a library.

ii. **responsibility** - personal and career development is largely determined by the performance, decisions and actions of the individual concerned; responsibility for planning work or learning activities which will enhance development lies primarily with the individual, **in partnership** with their manager or supervisor.

iii. **dependence on innovative and effective devolved management of staff resources -** Regional and local managers are in a position to influence approaches to and opportunities for development and training at all levels, in their allocation of staff resources within the funds available to them.

The LADP aims to provide a flexible framework which can be tailored to meet the needs of the individual and their workplace; it is structured primarily around workplace training, experience and assessment. This is supported by attendance on appropriate courses organised by the HLAI Training Office and at Regional/Community Library level.

The documentation that follows forms the basis of the Library Assistants' Development Programme (LADP) and a copy should be given to all new Library Assistants.

Example 6 continued

LIBRARY ASSISTANTS' DEVELOPMENT PROGRAMME (LADP)

Example 6   continued

Stage II

Library Assistants' Development Programme

Following completion of Induction training, all staff appointed at H2 are expected to gain practical experience and training in the areas on the following pages.

Supervision

The candidate will be supervised by her/his Line Manager or SLA or designated person responsible for training Library Assistants (see Appendix II for details of recommended training and/or experience for supervisors of candidates for the LADP). The supervisor will be able to assess the candidate more effectively by discussion about training and progress with other members of staff who have input into the training programme.

A meeting with the candidate to discuss their progress with the training programme should be arranged:

(i)   four months after appointment, in order to monitor progress and address any issues by the end of the statutory probation period (6 months).

(ii)   after 10 months from appointment to review and monitor progress, and to agree a possible completion date for the training programme with a view to applying for progression to H3. This meeting may be structured according to the guidelines for the Annual Development Review recommended for all staff. (see Appendix I)

Progression to H3

Progression to H3 will be conditional on the following:

i   The areas listed overleaf have constituted a regular (say, weekly opportunity) part of the candidate's duties over a period **of at least 3 months** prior to application for H3. (It is recognised that this condition may not realistically apply to all items on the checklist.)

ii   The candidate has demonstrated both competence and confidence in carrying out all the duties relating to the areas of work in the checklist.

iii   The supervisor and the candidate are both satisfied that the above conditions (i) and (ii) have been met. This agreement should be sought at the Annual Development Review (or similar meeting at the appropriate time).

iv   The candidate has completed a minimum of 1 year's employment with HLAI. (For part time staff working less than 20 hours a week, this minimum period should realistically be 18 months.)

2

Example 6   continued

LADP STAGE II: TRAINING CHECKLIST FOR LIBRARY ASSISTANTS

Candidate's Name ....   Supervisor's Name.........................

Start date of Training Programme...................

AREA OF TRAINING	TRAINING PERIOD/ DATE	COMPETENCE CONFIDENCE ATTAINED	CANDIDATE'S SIGNATURE	MANAGER'S SIGNATURE
1. CUSTOMER CARE **Understanding and demonstration of:** - polite and friendly manner to members of the public - courtesy, patience and tact as required/appropriate - positive attitude to HLAI and HCC in dealings with the public - non-judgemental acceptance of customer needs - listening and communication skills face-to-face and on the telephone - basic structure of HLAI and Region				

4

Example 7

UNIVERSITY OF HUDDERSFIELD

LIBRARY SERVICES

EFFECTIVE TRAINING

AIM

To enable participants to effectively provide quality 'on the job' training to individuals and / or groups of two and three.

OBJECTIVES

By the end of the course participants can expect to have had the opportunity to:

- identify factors which affect learning and training e.g. environment, planning, prior knowledge of trainee, how people learn

- appraise methods of training, including how to reinforce learning, and training aids

- list and practise skills used in training in particular use of language both verbal and non verbal, giving and receiving feedback, planning

- consider ways of evaluating the effectiveness of training

The trainer is June Whetherly who looks forward to meeting you and working with you.

The course will be highly participative and experiential i.e. draw on your own experience. There will be opportunities to learn from exercises, discussion, role play, individual and small group work.

In preparation for the course you are asked to complete the attached learning styles questionnaire and bring it with you on the first day of the course. Also to identify at least one piece of on the job training you have or will be undertaking and be prepared to work with issues arising from this on the course. As there will be the opportunity on the second day to use this as a basis for practising what has been learnt on the course, please bring any visual or any other aids with you if this is practicable.

Example 7   continued

UNIVERSITY OF HUDDERSFIELD

LIBRARY SERVICES

EFFECTIVE TRAINING

PROGRAMME

DAY ONE

9.00	Introductions and course objectives
	Agreeing a learning contract
10.00	What is effective on the job training?
10.30	Coffee
10.45	Factors which affect training
	Preferred learning styles
12.30	Lunch
1.30	Training methods and aids/Reinforcing learning
3.00	Tea
3.15	Identifying and practising training skills
4.30	Review of day
5.00	Close

DAY TWO

9.00	Review
9.15	Further practise - feedback
10.30	Coffee
10.45	Planning training
12.30	Lunch
1.30	Pulling together what has been learnt
3.00	Tea
3.15	Evaluation of training
4.30	Review of course
5.00	Close

Example 7 continued

```
UNIVERSITY OF HUDDERSFIELD

EFFECTIVE TRAINING - EXTRACT FROM TRAINER'S PLAN

Overall   Time   Methods                          Media       What required of participants
time
---------------------------------------------------------------------------------------------------
9.00-     9.00-  Introduction by Asst. Head
10.00     9.10   Domestics / Quick round

          9.10-  Concerns / wants / hopes                     Pairs - listen to each other one at a
          9.25                                                time

          9.25-  Share in group                   Flipchart   Feedback what other said to group
          9.50

          9.50-  Offer a learning contract                    Agree a learning contract
          10.00

10.00-    10.00- What is on the job training?                 Discussion
10.30     10.20

          10.20- What makes it effective?
          10.30  Find out what on the job training
                 each person intends to do on this
                 course

10.30-           Coffee
10.45

10.45-    10.45- Exercise - worst teacher                     Pairs - talk about experience of worst
12.30     10.55                                               teacher + what stopped learning

          10.55- Plenary - share experiences
          11.05

          11.05- Exercise - best teacher                      Same pairs - experience + what enabled
          11.20                                               learning

          11.20- Plenary - share experiences
          11.30

          11.30- What other factors affect ability Flipchart  Discussion
          11.50  to learn?                         Checklist

          11.50- Introduce "Learning styles"
          12.00

          12.00- Mark questionnaires              Handouts    Individual work
          12.15

          12.15- Plenary - discuss outcomes
          12.30

12.30            Lunch
```

Example 8

STAFF DEVELOPMENT GUIDELINES

SHORT COURSES, CONFERENCES AND VISITS

1) <u>Finding out what courses are available</u>

Information about training is sent to all Library Staff Development Group representatives. Each person should make sure that their representative lets them see what's going to happen well in advance.

The Library Association Record and other professional publications often carry notification of future events. It helps if professional journals are circulated as quickly as possible.

Talk to people - someone else may have spotted just the course you think you need.

2) <u>Checking if you can attend</u>

Firstly, make sure the date fits in with other commitments and whether other staff will be able to cover your absence. Site Librarians must be consulted by <u>all</u> staff about any activity which involves time away from the Library.

Secondly, check that funding will be available, if applicable. You should check this with the Deputy Librarian (Personnel) before booking a place.

3) <u>Booking the course</u>

Book your own place on the course. If possible, request invoices to be marked for the attention of the Deputy Librarian (Personnel).

Fill in the appropriate form, attach any documentation about the course, and send it to Julie Parry. These forms constitute an important record of what courses and events have been attended. Please make sure you always submit one, even if no payment is involved.

All academic staff should use form SD1.

All APT&C staff should use the 3 part form headed APPLICATION FOR TRAINING COURSE/CONFERENCE.

4) <u>Travelling</u>

If you are planning to travel by train or coach you can get a ticket in advance by completing a UWE Union Travel Shop Voucher. Send the top two copies of the voucher to Julie Parry not more than one month and not less than one week before you intend to travel. Your ticket will be sent through the internal post.

Example 8   continued

The other option is to pay your own travelling expenses and claim afterwards using an EXPENSES CLAIM FORM - STAFF. For subsistence and car allowances there are set rates which should be available at each site.

5)   Evaluation of training: reports

It is a condition of attending such events that a report should be produced. The aims of such reports are
a)   to assess the value of the course;
b)   to assess the value to the individual of attending the course.
The information gained will enable us to obtain a clearer picture of the advantages which people, as individuals, feel they have gained from attending. We will also be able to identify which organisations run the most effective courses and those which are best avoided. Such information can then be used in the formation of future staff development policies.

Reports may be submitted in any format and will obviously vary in length, according to the nature of the event. However, each one must include the following:

Title of course
Organising body
Venue
Date(s)

Short abstract of the report

Description of the event

An evaluation of the event
      e.g. What was the organisation like?
           Was the content relevant/at the right level?
           What were the speakers like?
           Was there opportunity for discussion?
           Would you recommend it to others?
           Etc.

An assessment of its value to you
      e.g. How will it help you in your current work?
           How will it aid your future development?
           Was it stimulating/boring?
           Did you learn new things?
           Did you meet interesting colleagues?

Your report should be sent to Julie Parry within two months of the course. All reports are held in a central collection organised by Mary Exon. Anyone can request to see a report - simply contact Mary.

JP 16/12/92

Example 8   continued

STAFF DEVELOPMENT GUIDELINES

EXTENDED COURSES OF STUDY

The following guidelines refer to the funding and allowance of time off for extended courses of study. As the intention is to produce a system which is essentially equitable yet flexible, it is recognised that certain anomalies may occur. For example, two people could be following the same course but receive different levels of funding, depending on the vocational relevance of the subject. Therefore, the guidelines aim to focus on the needs of individuals rather than the intrinsic value of a course. Successful applications for funding are likely to be those relating to training needs which have already been discussed with managers, site librarians or other senior staff.

The following points apply in all cases:

1) These guidelines refer only to extended courses of part-time or distance learning study. They do not include short courses, conferences or full-time study.

2) The guidelines apply equally to both academic and APT&C staff.

3) The payment of fees and any other expenses will be discretionary and subject to availability of funds.

4) Time off for residential schools, exams etc. must be arranged in advance with the Site Librarian.

5) All courses of study where funding or time off is requested must be authorised by the Deputy Librarian (Personnel).

6) Any member of staff whose course is funded from central Polytechnic funds will be bound by the regulations in the Polytechnic's Scheme of financial assistance for training.

Professional courses

Description :   courses in Library and Information work.

Examples: City and Guilds Library Assistants' course, M.Lib.

Funding: 100% of course fees, up to a ceiling of £750 per person per year. Travel expenses to be assessed according to requirements.

Attendance: time off to be allowed to attend compulsory elements of the course e.g. day release or residential school.

Exams: one full day to be allowed for each exam i.e. whole day for an afternoon exam or previous afternoon and morning for a morning exam. One whole day per exam also allowed for revision, up to a maximum of 3 days.

Materials: text books etc. to be paid for by the individual concerned.

Example 8   continued

Professionally related course

Description: courses (other than those in Library and
Information work) relevant to the work currently
done by an individual or relevant to professional
development.

Examples: subject related courses for Subject Librarians;
general management courses.

Funding: a maximum of 75% of fees will be paid, up to a ceiling
of £450 per individual, per year. Travel expenses to
be assessed according to individual requirements.

Attendance: time off to be allowed to attend compulsory one-off
elements of the course e.g. residential school but
regular sessions, such as lectures, must be attended
in own time.

Exams: as above

Materials: as above

Personal development

Description: courses which lead to the personal development of
individuals but are not directly related to their
current work.

Examples: Open University degrees.

Funding: a maximum of 50% of fees will be paid, up to a ceiling
of £200. Travel expenses to be paid by the individual
concerned.

Attendance: time off will be allowed to attend compulsory one-off
elements of the course e.g. residential schools.
Regular commitments, such as lectures, to be attended
in own time.

Exams: as above

Materials: as above

Exclusions: whilst all courses leading to further qualifications
may be considered, funding will not be available for
"recreational" courses e.g. bricklaying, yoga,
windsurfing or car maintenance.

JP 16/12/92

Example 9

Training Events Checklist

Identified need?   Organisational / Personal Development

Set Objectives – agree with function Head if necessary

Identify speakers/tutors/facilitators and agree areas to be covered/methods to be used. Agree date.

Book venue! – and necessary equipment.

Confirm external speakers by letter, request equipment/other needs

Prepare publicity material – circulate to appropriate managers for approval if necessary.

Circulate publicity – with closing date for applications.

On/after closing date:- select participants if oversubscribed
- confirm successful participants
- write to unsucessful participants, include any plans to repeat event or alternatives if appropriate
- book refreshments

Write/copy exercises, handouts as appropriate, prepare badges if used

Confirm final arrangements with speakers, send programmes, maps and lists of participants, check details for reception.

On the day:- buy neccesary tea, coffee, etc – depends on venue arrangements
- get to venue early – check equipment (safety/working order/spare bulbs, etc)
- check fire exits / procedures, smoking policy in building, first aid provision.
- re-arrange room – if neccesary
- welcome participants with coffee/tea, arrange introductions if necessary, announce domestic arrangements – smile!

Follow up –   check evaluation (formal/informal)
–   any further needs arising?
–   need to repeat?

Example 10

UNIVERSITY OF NOTTINGHAM

LIBRARY

APPLICATION TO ATTEND EXTERNAL COURSE/CONFERENCE/VISIT

PART I   NAME

            LIBRARY

            EXT

NAME OF EVENT

VENUE

INCLUSIVE DATES ABSENT FROM NOTTINGHAM

NUMBER OF WORKING DAYS ABSENT

REASONS FOR ATTENDING

a) BENEFIT TO YOU

b) BENEFIT TO THE LIBRARY

COSTS

£

    − Conference/course fee

    − Estimated travel/subsistence costs

I support this application to attend   <u>TOTAL</u>   £ _____

Signed.............. (Library Manager/section head)

PASS TO DEPUTY LIBRARIAN, HALLWARD LIBRARY, WITH A COPY OF COURSE/CONFERENCE DETAILS FILLED OUT (ie. assume application will be successful)

Agreement to attend/incur expenses ....
                                     (Deputy Librarian)

<u>NB</u> Pass any invoices received IMMEDIATELY to DEPUTY LIBRARIAN for payment.

This form will be returned to you - please retain it until after the event.

Example 10 **continued**

PART II

Pass to your library manager **within seven days** of return from the event.

1. **BRIEF REPORT** (Unless you specifically ask otherwise, this **may** be printed in the **Library Newsletter**).

2. **ASSESSMENT OF BENEFIT**

    a)   **Benefit to you**

    b)   **Benefit to the library**

    c)   **Would you recommend that someone else go?**

3. **EXPENSES**

    Enclose: - Completed University expenses claim form (keep the second copy for your reference);
    - invoices
    - receipts (not usually needed for travel).

    Reimbursement is usually made quickly. (Finance Office will pay cash if you wish - if you do, indicate on this form and the blue form will be returned to you).

    SEND TO: **DEPUTY LIBRARIAN, HALLWARD LIBRARY**

    RO 9.92

Index